THE HAUNTED DOLPHIN HOTEL

Voted No.1 most haunted venue by the public's Most Haunted Experience

Written by
Wendy Jack

....do you dare to be scared...

www.facebook.com/WendyJack, Clairvoyant and Psychic Medium

wendy-jack@sky.com

Thank you to Ellie Boiling for providing photographic evidence, and the history of The Dolphin Hotel. The endless phone calls and video chats while editing, re-writing, grammar policing, going through thousands of photos, videos and screenshots and the encouragement you gave while writing The Haunted Dolphin Hotel. We did it!

The countless ghost hunts, the laughs as you have gone screaming out of the door, the goose bumps, scary moments, and at times the totally unexplainable events that have happened. The old Dolly with her spiritual guests performed to their fullest, making people's experiences exceptional. Thank you to the guests, punters and ghost hunters who shared their experiences while visiting The Dolphin Hotel, without the input from Ellie and all of you this would not have been possible. One day soon there will be many more ghost hunts to come once COVID 19 has passed, until then I hope you enjoy reading this as much as I did writing it. Prepare to be scared....or somewhat intrigued...

Wendy Jack x

Ode to the Dolly

The Dolly stands tall and proud
Upon the corner of hope and dreams,
Many a footfall has tread upon her boards
Some still dwell within the walls so it seems.
The foundations echo with tears of sorrow
On the dawning of this sad day,
The rooms stand silent, laughter and joy no longer
Left within the hands of come what may.
Once a thriving port of call
As a livery, hotel, garage, and pub,
Regulars came from near and far
To a place full of compassion, warmth, and love.
Even though inside it is devoid of the living
There remains the spirit of the dead,
To walk the stairs, floors, and bars still today
Caught within the time of the life they led.
Whispers, giggles, singing, and apparitions
With many a spooky going on,
The 'children' playing hide and seek
As the smugglers sing their sailor songs.
Many a deceased landlord still stays and linger
Waiting for the paying fare,
Once normality has been restored
We hope to see you there....

WENDY JACK

CONTENTS

FOREWORD

'What can I say about this wonderful, old building, my pride, my joy, and home for 20 years? The Dolphin is a unique, quirky, and sometimes a petrifying place to live and work. I will never get used to all the spiritual activity that happens here, how could I? We are dealing with a different realm and although I have been a paranormal investigator for nearly 30 years, The Dolphin packs such a paranormal punch that sometimes it takes your breath away.

A big thank you to Wendy Jack for writing this fantastic tribute to The Old Dolly, I will treasure it always....

.....do you dare to be scared?'

Ellie Boiling x

INTRODUCTION

This book has been written to share publications, weird, wonderful, and questionable experiences that many have witnessed when crossing over the threshold of The Dolphin Hotel. As a clairvoyant and psychic medium, I also wanted to share my experiences and bring to light what others have felt, seen, heard, smelt, tasted, with a sense of knowing, as a punter, guest, worker, and well-known ghost hunters who have tried to lift the skirt on the old Dolly to find out what lies beneath. Here are a few highlights with many more endless tales still waiting to be told. Whether you are a sceptic or not, the amount of evidence that has been witnessed not just by one person but by many groups has been so overwhelming it could not be dismissed anymore. Those of you who are thinking, yeah right! I suggest you look at the written evidence, videos stills, and photographs, some of which you will find at the back of this book, caught at various times on ghost hunts, by chance or recorded on live feeds. Before Ellie became landlady of The Dolphin there were many stories handed down, were they true-life experiences or myths?... Only you can decide that. One thing is for sure; once you visit The Dolphin for longer than a quick beer it will make you question the possibilities of life after death. I for one know that when our bodies can no longer support a living soul it is never goodbye.... Just see you later.....

CHAPTER 1

The Dolphin Hotel

L et us turn back the hands of time in one of the most his-
torically, active buildings in England, voted No 1 most
haunted venue in December 2019 by the public through the
Most Haunted Experience. Built in 1735, The Dolphin Hotel
formerly known as The Dolphin Inn is situated on the corner of
High Street and Surrey Street, in Littlehampton, West Sussex.
Seven bedrooms full of history, energized by the spiritual residue that keeps a pulse still vibrating through the walls. Cellars
awash with active presence and corridors lined with the souls
and laughter of children. The toilets surprisingly can smell of
apple pie, however, the cook who dwells there is not so welcoming. Not surprising; since she left the earth plane without
her consent. The Dolphin has become famous for its spiritual
activity and I do not mean those behind the bar. This journey of
insight shows you the history behinds the activity that can be
witnessed today.

The Dolphin has many skeletons and I do not mean hypothetically! Some of which have been found. During my experiences,
the spirits wish to be heard, by allowing the secrets hidden
within the walls of The Dolphin to unfold, perhaps it will help
them to find peace; this is the spirits telling their tale.

The residential spiritual bad boy William will keep you on your
toes if you ever visit, you may feel him standing just a little
too close for comfort as you can feel his breath in your ear, but
be aware they are not sweet nothings he wants to whisper. His
favourite hobby was rape and murder; he still protests his innocence today. I am sure young Jane, his victim, will tell you a
thing or two, as she tends to be close by and often tells her tale
on the Ouija boards situated around The Dolphin. On still, dark,

nights her screams can still be heard within these walls.

There is a lot of controversy about Ouija boards, if you go looking for trouble especially from the dark side, you will find it and I do not mean in a good way. If you are pure of heart and work with love and light, your guides will surround you with protection. However, the most important thing is being with an experienced medium or Empath. Having the ability to sense the energies both positive and negative it enables you to tune into the spirits coming through, it is an excellent tool for communication when used in the right way. It is not for the inexperienced, to have a laugh with or to do when having your friends round for a beer because believe it or not, beer and spirits do not mix! You will end up with more than you bargained for, all communication needs to be opened and closed properly.

The landlady Ellie used to have a stall in The Dolphin called Pillywiggins with all things spiritual on display until a flood in the cellar damage all the stock, everything except for the Ouija Boards that is! Was it spirits way of getting the attention so they could be heard? That is why today you will find them scattered around the hotel in case you fancy a chat!

There are many rooms with nooks and crannies with secrets to be told where you can stumble across a disembodied spirit or 10. The remains of a woman can be found behind the wall in the cellar, so the spirits say, along with the drunken sailors crushed in the smuggling tunnels in the foundations beneath...The song 'What has become of the drunken sailor' will be in your head by the time you leave ......'as the rocks came crashing down!'

The dumbwaiter was not only used for food, allegedly the bodies of two small, lost souls were found inside. Children's laughter can still be heard as they continue to play hide and seek but never can be found. If you listen carefully in the cellar you can hear the thud of them falling to their deaths.

Rumour has it tiny bones were found in a chimney from a sweep that never finished his shift!

The Gentleman's Club was a secret society that held onto their privacy, only the elite could join. However, spirit has no class; privacy is not something they uphold. What dark secrets will they unveil? You will have to wait and see.

Hanging seemed to be a past time for an old landlord and Molly the good-time girl whose advances were rejected. They like to show what it feels like to be hung, so if you visit please do tell if you cannot breathe, preferably before you turn blue...

Each room has a spiritual ambiance as various living occupants have experienced, including one couple who fled in the middle of the night without even a goodbye. How rude! They did, however, inform a national newspaper. Apparently having your duvet turned down in the middle of the night while in the bed was just too much room service. Especially as the lady in white did not use the door to enter or leave and gave a whole new meaning to the word legless.

Be mindful of standing too close to the windows you may just be pulled out. One lady who used to work at The Dolphin felt compelled to jump out of the window as a previous landlord had done before, a broken leg was not what she had bargained for, the landlord was not so lucky!

Blunt head trauma is another favourite these spirits like to give so do have your paracetamol handy when visiting, as they tend to share the pain.

Fredrick is another bad boy who loiters, growls and rolls his barrels, a lot! Conversation is obviously not his strongest attribute.

The children, there are so many who have died for various reasons including the plague, influenza, consumption, diphtheria, thyroid, fire, etc. The Dolphin cellar which is also known as the Coffin Room was used as an overflow for the morgue during epidemics. The sound of them singing 'ring a ring a roses' with the emphases on 'we all fall down,' can often be heard. Giggling, balls bouncing, skipping, hair and clothes being pulled can also be heard and felt by these playful souls, so there is never a dull moment. The most famous child of all is Little Dolly, named after the nickname of The Dolphin Hotel, who had previously been accused of being a demon by a TV show that was filmed at The Dolphin. There is so much positive evidence about this little girl; I feel she was just misunderstood.

Many a celebrity has stayed at The Dolphin Hotel including Lord Byron and Oliver Reed who was kicked out in 1971 for being drunk and disorderly, surprisingly! Benny Hill and Anna Neagle to name but a few who are now in spirit tend to pop back for a little R and R, well I am sure their spiritual duties can be exhausting at times! Due to the regular ghost hunts, psychic circles, and live feeds on Facebook held in The Dolphin, they like to make an appearance to be remembered now and then. The autograph signing is a lot to be desired!

This is just the tip of the iceberg with murders, suicides, and just the unexplained. The Dolphin has been featured in Chats Fate and Fortune, Take a Break, and Love It! magazines, in books and newspapers and on radio shows on more than one occasion. Famous mediums Derek Acorah in TV's Ghost Towns and Colin Fry have visited. TV crews including Fred Batt from Most Haunted and Barri Ghai from Help! My House Is Haunted has also visited. Paranormal investigators have all come to explore the secrets of The Dolphin to be met with spiritual energies both good and bad. Little Dolly who was accused of being a negative black-eyed child in spirit, whose grave can be found in a local cemetery has popped in when they have been visiting. Many have left looking over their shoulders when leaving, to ensure the Demons they sensed have been left behind within the walls of The Dolphin, with the only thing they are taking home is their equipment. The thousands of lost souls remain in the ever-revolving spiritual door, the red portal fondly known as The Devils Gate which brings in an array of different spirits all the time. The portal is huge and the spirits do not wish to leave, so it tends to attract more.

There is not a day that goes by without the spiritual residents of

The Dolphin letting their presence be known; they often pop in to say hello. There are video frames and picture evidence some of which you will find further in the book, you can also go to The Haunted Dolphin Hotel or The L.I.G.H.T Paranormal Team on Facebook for live video evidence on ghost hunts. This is their home. As the years fall away within the walls of The Dolphin Hotel the creaks and groans of the floorboards once trodden by the spirits of today in the past long since forgotten. They continue to live their lives trapped by the fear of perhaps retribution for their sins or fear of the unknown. If you decide to visit, open up to spirit rather than be blinkered, you may even feel them near, reliving memories, hear the laughter and chatter of conversations that have been left in the distance past, moments like a snapshot in time. Allow them to come through, see their faces, hear their voices, the chatter of adults, and the laughter of children, hear what they have to say, let them know they are being thought of encouraging them to come forward. Listen carefully, engage fully with an open mind as negativity can stop them from trying to communicate, speak clearly and loudly, for the energy generated by your voice helps them to come through, this is not just for The Dolphin Hotel, but around you wherever you may be, you may find the medium in you yet.

If you are passing, the food is delicious, the hospitality is amazing, enjoy, stay safe, perhaps bring a crystal or two to hold on tight for protection. Oh and by the way don't go anywhere alone; otherwise, you may just end up staying at The Dolphin Hotel ...... permanently!

Now we have skimmed the surface, let us go a little deeper into the old Dolly...

CHAPTER 2

Once visited never forgotten

S tanding in front of The Dolphin supercharged energy filled the air before I had even stepped foot inside, every window was full of children looking out. This may not seem unusual except the children I could see had long since passed and now The Dolphin was their forever home. This was the first time I had ever stepped inside to meet my friend Jackie Dann for lunch.

Just a little insight, even though I only live a few miles away I tend to live in my little bubble of spiritual development. Playing in a graveyard opposite my house normally on my own as a child was nothing unusual to me. However, many would care to differ. As I grew older my psychic and mediumship abilities began to intensify until having a conversation with a passing spirit or two became the norm for me. Learning self-protection and joining psychic circles to enhance my gift ultimately lead me to become a full-time medium. I work on behalf of various famous mediums, TV stations, and magazines giving readings all over the world after showing my abilities by completing a three-hour working interview. I also conduct spiritual church services and demonstrations, ghost hunts, run two psychic circles to help people develop their gift, house clearings of negative energies, poltergeist and active spirits, portal closings, and cleansing auras by moving on attachments, all of which are a daily event for me. I do not fear the dead as I work with love and light and only positivity, it's the living you need to watch out for.

Now, of course, many people will read this and think what a load of rubbish, but let me just put this out there... I give readings to people over the telephone that I cannot see, I ask for their first name and date of birth that is all. Try Googling Tracey born in 1982! I do not want information, for people to 'feed the medium'. I then tell them what I am being told by their loved ones in spirit with the help of my guides; after all, I am just the messenger. People come back to me time and time again so I know I must be doing something right. I have no way of knowing the information that I am giving, which they tell me is accurate. Spirit also give advice, how to change your life and the potential outcomes. Freedom of choice, stubbornness, and denial can stop people from achieving these things and potential predictions coming true, timings can also be changed or delayed. People can be very quick to blame the medium rather than look inside themselves. Of course, there are charlatans as in any industry, when choosing a medium go by recommendations, do not give any information and if they are vague end the session so you do not have to pay for something that does not make you feel as if you have had a good reading. There can be times when spirits will not read for a person, here are a few of the reasons: they may be overly stressed or mentally upset, spirits may feel it is not the right time for them to have a reading, they may not be open to receiving messages from spirit and lack understanding of the significance of what is being said, they go for too many readings or people just do not listen to the advice given by spirit even when they are told the same thing over and over again.

Mediums should not tell you anything bad; when you or the people close to you are going to die it is not their job to tell you. Curses only seem to work if you believe them and anyone looking for vast amounts of money while you have to do ridiculous rituals avoid like the plague.

Working as a medium I have an open mind, every medium works differently. I use all the senses: see, hear, feel, taste, touch and smell everything to do with spirit, possess a sense of knowing, intuition and empathic to the point that I can feel how people passed. Even with the living, especially when they are feeling unwell or going through emotional trauma, I feel a tornado of feelings which are not mine; previously working as a counsellor and psychotherapist was a nightmare. Not only would I feel what was going on for them, but I would also see all of their relatives who had passed coming along for support. Now that for me was intimidating, one person in the chair with their whole deceased family looking at you, no pressure! Many mediums start as counsellors because they are empathic to people's emotions.

Spirit work with mediums in different ways utilising their strengths by using signs and symbols which then need to be interpreted, sometimes it can be misunderstood at first but as time unfolds it becomes clear. After all, we are communicating through a three-way intercom system that can have interference, especially if the spirit is inexperienced in communicating or just plain bloody-minded. You can get mischievous, playful, negative, arrogant, stubborn, difficult, angry, quiet, charming, funny, and just plain grumpy spirits, depending on how they were on the earth plane and that is exactly how they can come through. The worst kinds are the malevolent entities, these are dark energies that have not necessarily lived in human form but can cause havoc for some unsuspecting souls. Some spirits are just stuck because they are told 'when you are dead, you're dead!' They are too afraid to go to the light. Others think they have done wrong on earth and feel they will be held accountable for their actions so prefer to stay in familiar surroundings. Due to the number of spirits that are stuck on the earth plane not knowing what to do and want to try to live as they did when they were alive, they can sit in people's auras. This can result in people not feeling themselves, unexplained illnesses, feeling tired and fatigued especially if a person is feeling unwell and possess a complete change of character, for example, a once outgoing person can become sullen and withdrawn. Some mediums may have different points of view and disagree with what I am saying, however, over 50 something years later and I feel my information has served me well, after all, it is my guides who give it to me.

Just to define the difference between a ghost and a spirit: a ghost follows the path they know, a moment in time stuck on replay, a spirit is an energy force that interacts with the living.

I want to stress at this point that when people pass, their loved ones in spirit come forward to greet them so please do not think that they died alone, ultimately, it is up to them to decide if they go with them into the spirit realm. The shock of passing, not realising they have died, and how they passed can render them stuck on the earth plane. They can still have the ability to cross over even if it is not at the time of passing but when they are ready, that is where mediums and lightworkers come in to help spirit pass into the light. Perhaps if we look at it another way regardless of your beliefs especially after seeing SYFY movies, if an unexplainable light was coming down from the sky above you, would you run away or go with it?

As I have said before people say 'when you are dead you're dead!' Here is a thought: we have so much knowledge gained from lessons we have learned in life for our light to just be distinguished when our bodies can no longer function. It seems such a waste and rather naive to think this, especially if you believe in Albert Einstein's theory that items and buildings hold on to vibrations and energy which cannot be destroyed, therefore are eternal. So why not the human soul after all it is an energy force? There are many things in life that cannot necessarily be explained with science, so keep an open mind, do not judge other people's beliefs just because they do not agree with your own, being blinkered can close you down to so many possibilities, expect the unexpected, the signs are there.

Recently there have been so many children born that are able to see relatives that have died or have memories of their past lives, these are called indigo children. They seem to know things and can draw places, faces, and give information without prior knowledge. How is this possible? It is worth watching 'Ghost

Inside My Child', and then you can perhaps nurture a child's gift rather than dismiss it. There was also a feature recently in 2014 of a boy who took people to his killer from a previous life as an adult:

3-yr-old recalls past life, identifies killer, and location of the body

The Syrian boy, born with a long, red birthmark on his forehead, showed the elders where his past life's body and the murder weapon were buried.

A three-year-old boy in Syria's Golan Heights region had become the centre of attention after he revealed that he was murdered with an axe in his previous life.

The boy, of the Druze ethnic group, was born with a long, red birthmark on his head. According to Druze beliefs, birthmarks are related to past-life deaths. When the boy was old enough to talk, he told his family that he had been killed with an axe blow to his head.

As is the custom, the elders took the child to the home of his previous life to see if he remembered it, and sure enough, the boy knew the village he was from and once he arrived there, he remembered the name he had been given in his past life.

Locals told the elders that the man who the boy was claiming to be had gone missing four years earlier. When asked, the boy also remembered the full name of his killer. When the alleged killer was confronted, his face turned white, but he did not admit to murder.

The boy then took the elders to where the body was buried and in that very spot, they found a man's skeleton with a wound to the head that corresponded with the boy's birthmark, they also recovered the axe with which he had been killed. Faced with the evidence, the killer then admitted to the crime.

The boy's full story has been documented in the book, "Children

Who Have Lived Before: Reincarnation Today" by German therapist Trutz Hardo. ... Just saying... keep an open mind!

Anyhow, I am sure I will fill you in with more information as we travel back in time and explore the history and spiritual activity of The Dolphin and the land on which it is built.

Littlehampton was not a place I would frequent until I had given a reading to Jackie who invited me to lunch at The Dolphin Hotel. Full of excitement, she could not wait for me to feel the energy and to meet the landlady of this intriguing and busy pub; I do not mean only a place for the living! I was not sure exactly where it was but once I reached Littlehampton in West Sussex, the red portal of light emitting from the building was evident. Portals are through which spirit travel and can be various colours, blue and golden being the purest and positive energies, green is very much to do with nature especially in forest and wooded areas and red which is negative. Who needs a map when you have a beacon of red light glowing over a building? Miraculously, on a one-way system, on the busy high street, there was a parking space just outside, spirit knew I was coming.

To a sensitive like myself, you can feel the vibrations and energy bouncing off the walls before you even reach the building itself, for not only is there a past within the walls but also from the land it is built upon.

Going in the side door on the corner of the building you enter a mix of carpet and floorboards with a seated area surrounded by memorabilia of the past, each with a story to tell. There is also a slightly raised area with Union Jack flags and RAF, Army and Navy uniforms from the past and present surrounded by more tables and chairs.

Once inside the hands of time went into reverse as I could see how The Dolphin used to look as the memories within the walls started to come alive. The images I see play like a video in my head; these are the memories of spirit as they show me snippets of past events. The Dolphin transformed into a livery, coaching inn and stables. I could see horses eating out of troughs, wooden sawdust-covered floors, dogs, cats, and birds including a parrot flying through, in fact, an array of spiritual animals. Various people started to come in going through their motions like an old movie playing as they went about their business until it became The Dolphin looking how it was when it was first built. The landlord who I now know to be Fred Holliss was standing behind the bar smiling, in a loose-fitting white shirt, a serving girl walking around the customers laughing and talking as she went, a nun even floated past with a disdained look upon her face. By this time I was sitting at the table just inside the door giving a running commentary to the people who I had never met before but would be lunching with today. It was at this time I was aware of a little girl standing at the end of the table, I described her in detail only to be met with a resounding, "That's Dolly" by them all. A little boy joined Dolly and promptly twisted his ears and stuck his tongue out, charming! Spirit can tell who is spiritually aware because their auras have particular colours and glow so spirits are drawn to this. At that moment many more children started coming into where we were sitting, at this point I could also hear an accordion playing, joining in with the laughter and chatter of not only the living but the dead. At this point, Jackie said, "You will have to meet Ellie and tell her what you are seeing." I continued with my lunch all the while going through the symptoms of a heart attack, struggling to breathe, blunt head trauma to the head, coughing, being hung, you name the illness, death, and emotion and I was feeling it. I could also smell burning and hearing the word ashes to ashes, dust to dust. My guides were certainly working overtime to take the sensations away as they are there to protect me from overwhelming sensations and emotions.

Everyone has guides but those who work with spirit are given more spiritually advanced guides to help deliver messages and give healing. The amount of guides you have depends on the degree with which you work with spirit. They can change as the more advanced you become. Spirit workers may communicate with all their guides or just have one who gives them the information; it depends on how we connect with them. I like to talk with all of mine and know how they lived on the earth plane before they became spiritual guides.

The lunchtime session came to an end and the chef who is also the landlady approached our table, this is when I first met Ellie Boiling. Jackie asked me to tell Ellie all that I had seen and felt, so I described everything to her, she then said, "There is no way you could have known half the information, especially about the accordion as it had been stolen a few months back." Ellie has a book of pictures drawn by a spirit artist medium that had been in The Dolphin, I had described the contents of the book along with the deaths I had experienced before she had even shown it to me. It is at this point that Ellie felt I was the real deal, empathic to spirit herself; we arranged a guided tour of The Dolphin to see what else I could pick up.

A week later *pendulum in my hand, fondly named Penji, we started on our tour of what I now felt was a very active hotel full of rape, murder, betrayal, and secrets that would make your hair curl. A mixture of spiritual energies and negativity that would make the film The Omen look like a Disney remake, starting with...... Actually, why not read for yourself as the stories, information and the history of The Dolphin unfold and see what you make of it!

*Definition of a pendulum for spiritual work: they can come in various shapes and sizes, ideally with a pointed crystal on the end of a small chain that can be held in between the thumb and forefinger. Normally there is a small ball on the end which allows the crystal to swing freely, dispelling beliefs that people move it themselves. It works with the energy field around our aura; the more spiritual you are the more it swings and can give simple yes or no answers once you define the movement of the pendulum. It can also locate items and spell out letters and words when used on an Angel board. I use a wax cord necklace with a chunk of amethyst on the end which I wear all the time. Of course, working with a spirit you can get mischievous energies that can give false answers, the more you work with the pendulum the more you know, sense and feel the energy when the answers given are right or if they are wrong. Armed with Penji the information was revealed....

CHAPTER 3

Ellie Boiling

Ellie originally started work at The Dolphin from 1988-1989 as a part-time chef. Ellie lived in room 2 with a work colleague staying in room 1. Nearly every room in the hotel has experienced spiritual activity of some kind which has been documented in various capacities throughout time. For Ellie, below is the first of many weird, wacky, and just plain scary, underwear changing experiences she has felt, heard, and seen ever since she stepped over the threshold of The Dolphin Hotel.

Late one night whilst in her room, Ellie heard a loud scream, confused about where it was coming from Ellie knocked on the door of the part-time barmaid who lived in room 1. The door was already ajar, walking inside Ellie found the window wide open with the curtains billowing in the breeze. Looking out, Ellie found the barmaid had thrown herself out of the window and was now lying in the hotel gardens where a wooden gazebo now stands, with her leg positioned in a sickening, unnatural position. Ellie screamed and went to her aid thinking that she was attempting to take her own life. While waiting for the ambulance Ellie asked her what had happened, the barmaid said that she had no recollection as to why she had done it other than this overwhelming feeling of being compelled to jump from the window.

In a documented newspaper clipping from 1947, an open verdict was recorded on landlord Fredrick Henry Holliss's death after being found dying at the rear of the hotel. His widow had said her husband had been ill for the last 3 months; she had called the doctor after he was found wandering on Monday evening muttering incoherently about cats on the wardrobe.

She stayed with him until 3 am when he appeared to be sleeping. At 5.45 am the local milkman, Leonard Anstiss said that when he reached the area of The Dolphin he heard a man groaning, on striking a match he found Fredrick lying in his pyjamas. The reason why he jumped no one knows exactly. Financially he was comfortable, but he had recently been given notice to leave The Dolphin. Was this enough reason for him to jump out of the window to his death? Or was spiritual energies at play and The Dolphin did not want to lose such a popular and well known landlord? Are the residual energies and emotions he felt still within the walls? Were they responsible for not only Fredrick jumping out of the window but for luring another poor soul to join him in the same way? Was he trying to tell the tale of how he died? Luckily, the barmaid only ended up with a broken leg, unfortunately, Fredrick was not so lucky.

Ellie had visited the barmaid in hospital and confirmed that she was not an excessive drinker, was emotionally stable, had no desire or intention to harm herself before, and could not fathom out why she would open the window and jump out. Strangely, she somehow managed to land in exactly the same spot as the landlord did in 1947.

Ellie, after being as fit as a fiddle became continually ill with one illness after another including severe psoriasis, tonsillitis, glandular fever, food poisoning, and kidney infection causing excessive blood loss all within three months. Finding it increasingly more difficult to work and live there Ellie decided to move out and her health immediately improved. Were the negative energies at play once again, especially as the past is littered with documented unexplained sightings, events, and sensations?

Ellie then left completely, pursuing a military career, at that point in her life she was back to her old self but it seemed that the old Dolly was not done with Ellie yet.

In 1993-1995 Ellie returned to The Dolphin again working as a chef but this time did not live there. The energies of The Dolphin once again took their toll on Ellie so she left and went to work in the Cob & Pen which was actually the original Dolphin Pub, situated at the other end of Surrey Street. I'll explain the history behind this in the next chapter which is an intriguing tale within itself. She also worked in The Crown along with a few other places but could not seem to settle as The Dolphin Hotel was still always in the back of her mind. It seemed as if the universe was forcing Ellie's hand. Things started to go wrong without a clearly defined reason why leading Ellie to hit rock bottom.

In the year 2000, Ellie found herself homeless, with no money she had been wandering from place to place. While Ellie was sitting on some steps at St. Catherines Road in Littlehampton, a man was starring at Ellie, when she asked, "What are you looking at?" He walked away and then came back after 10 minutes, touched her on the head and gave her a £5 note, a bottle of lemonade and a piece of cake and said, "God bless you, you will find the strength today to climb out of this hole." He then walked away never to be seen again. Ellie then walked into town and saw in the window an advert for a part-time chef at The Dolphin Hotel, she immediately walked in and interviewed for the position. The job was hers and she started work the next day which again was a live-in job. Perhaps divine intervention or The Dolphin bringing one of its flock back home? Only the universe knows the answer.

There were a few things in The Dolphin at that time which was questionable with some of the locals and staff. Things needed to change and behaviour addressed. After talking with the then landlord, Ellie was made manager but things still needed tweaking, after many a discussion with the brewery and the police. Ellie was given the opportunity to take on the lease and become the landlady and finally put down roots but with the understanding that all negative behaviour had to stop otherwise, she would lose her home. Due to lack of funds, she needed a backer and this is where it starts to get a little weird, a man came forward telling Ellie that he has always wanted a pub, he would be the silent partner in a business venture where he would be the guarantor and financial backer. At this time he was applying to be a licensee, his behaviour started to change along with the probability that even though she was still the manager, Ellie would have been cast aside once he had taken over. The day before he was due to get the licence he was pulled over for driving under the influence, the chances of him getting a licensee after that was non-existent. When Ellie found out and asked him about what had happened, he didn't answer and just disappeared leaving the stock and furniture but took his investment, never to be seen again!

Now things get weirder still. Faced with no guarantor and no financial backing Ellie went back again to the brewery. This time they offered her the lease which she would have to pay back, but she would have to find a bond of £3000 first. Elated and mortified at the same time she got off the phone knowing she had no hope of ever getting together £3000. However, sitting in the bar was a lady who had a disabled child that Ellie had organised a party for. The woman had overheard Ellie's telephone conversation with the brewery and being so grateful for her kindness, offered to loan her the money for the bond. Ellie was speechless and believe me being speechless is not one of her traits as people who know her well would swiftly agree! She paid the bond, signed the lease, and at last, The Dolphin Hotel was hers. With not a penny to her name, she was elated the hotel was finally in her hands. Ellie went to pay the lady back £200 a month, imagine her surprise when the lady told her, "I don't want it, my brother has just died in Australia and has left me loads of money so God bless you, it's yours."

A series of extraordinary events that led to Ellie being the owner, was it Ellie's doing or a higher force?

Ellie had been a paying customer since 1985, was The Dolphin's house Pool champion, she was the only woman in the team and ended up beating all the men, (sorry just had to put that in being a pool player myself in my youth) she remembers thinking to herself that wouldn't it be lovely to own this pub one day. She had heard the rumours that The Dolphin was haunted from the locals, of glasses and bottles being chucked off the shelf, they also made a throwaway comment about old Tom talking to someone in the bar but no one was there. Ellie thought they were pulling her leg as she was so young at the time. Events soon changed her mind when odd things started happening while she worked for Chris and Matt in 1988, but she still did not really take it too seriously. Feeling the energies within The Dolphin it fascinated her to the point of being respectful and passionate about the building and all who dwelled there, the living and the dead. Perhaps The Dolphin was listening!

Being empathic to spirit herself since childhood; Ellie saw her father who had died when she was 6 years old, and when she was 9 he showed himself to her again. Even at that early age, Ellie questioned if she had seen him and did not take too much notice of her ability until later. It was when her mother, who was a spiritualist and healer, was giving Ellie her weekly hands-on healing that she suddenly started to see bright colours through her psychic third eye. She then started hearing marching boots, but she did not understand the significance. Ellie asked her mother why she was now seeing marching boots passing, then a blonde man marching with his unit who was looking straight at her, smiling. He then went around a corner and pointed towards a signpost. Her mother asked, "What was on the sign?" Ellie replied, "C.A.E.N," which is in France.

Ellie's mum had a dilly dalliance with a French-Canadian soldier in the war that was posted in her village. When she was 9 months pregnant she waved him off at the train station and her last words to him were, "Do not get killed." They were not married at the time so any telegram that would have been sent would have gone to his mother in Canada with all the information on where and how he was killed. Ellie's mum asked her to describe what the soldier looked like and Ellie promptly told her what she could see and a full description of him. Her mother was shocked and said, "Oh my god that sounds like Gilbert!" She then gave all the information to Ellie's sister, Gilbert's daughter, who then managed to use it to trace her family in Canada, she still sees them today. A family she may never have found if it was not for Ellie's vision. This was Ellie's first experience using her psychic eye, spirit work in mysterious ways.

Over the years Ellie tends to feel rather than see and it has only recently come to light that due to autism and Aspergers, it limits her psychic visual abilities. The experience along with the events that were happening in The Dolphin ignited her passion for the supernatural and the reason why she started up The L.I.G.H.T Paranormal Team in 2006. At this point, the activity in The Dolphin had eased a little, maybe because they trusted Ellie, so with Mark Green, who is still in the group today, and two other founding members Elaine and Brenda they concentrated on hauntings in private houses, haunted woods, UFO and extraterrestrial, as well as conducting 4 big public ghost hunts a year at The Dolphin. More information can be found in chapter 13.

The very first time Ellie had something significant happen to her that she experienced was in 2007. It was as if The Dolphin was biding its time. Ellie and her then fiancé together ran The Dolphin Hotel as a busy B&B, they had settled down to go to sleep having checked out all of the guests and prepared it for the new arrivals the next day. At the time there was absolutely no one staying in the building. Startled awake by the sound of running up and down in the top corridor which runs alongside the private residence, it was then followed by a loud noise coming from directly above them. They both sat bolt upright and thought someone had broken in and did not think for one second it was spiritual activity. Ellie got the base ball bat by her side and her partner got the torch, it was 3 am! They both went to investigate and Ellie shouted out, "If anyone is there I suggest you go out the same way as you came in as the police have been called, no harm will come to you." With other chosen choice words that may be too offensive for your delicate eyes! As they were going up the corridor towards room 7, they could hear things including banging, a child laughing behind them and whispering along with footsteps, turning around there was nothing there. Ellie had never been so scared in her whole life, after checking all of the rooms and finding nothing at all they quickly ran back to the flat until the morning. They soon concluded that what they experienced was something paranormal, there were alarms everywhere and CCTV that would have captured someone, no one alive could have got into the building.

Ellie's partner had previously experienced something in 2006 which made her doubt herself and what she had seen. Ellie asked her if she could clean room 4 as the client had left that morning, taking all the cleaning equipment upstairs she knocked on the door just to make sure no one was inside. From outside the door she could hear talking, thinking the client had come back because he had forgotten something, she opened the door to find a spirit standing in front of her who then seemed to walk straight through her. Absolutely petrified from this experience she could not stop shaking, she was continually being sick and ended up taking 2 days off. Once Ellie's fiancé had calmed down she explained what she had seen, her description of the gentleman is as follows; he was tall, really thin, with sunken dark cheeks, bald head and dark full beard. The gentleman who had checked out had grade 3 cropped hair and was short, hardly twins! Why did she stay? Well we tend to second guess ourselves and question what we saw and then talk ourselves out of what actually happened.

Before this, it was just little things that couldn't be explained, items would go missing, things would be moving and chucked, the gas was being played with and barrels being uncoupled in the cellar, they were starting to question their sanity. One very weird event in The Dolphin was experienced by some customers, 20p pieces where literally like pennies from heaven. A sealed off hatchway was chucking down these coins onto regulars standing at the bar, so intense was the force with which they were thrown it caused a scar on one lady's chest which can still be seen today, this was reported in the local paper which can be found at the end. After that things just got progressively worse on a daily basis and became more frequent. The customers used to tell Ellie about being hit, poked, and shoved with things being thrown at them. The more customers Ellie spoke to, especially the ones that were regulars from the '50s and '60s, the more things came to light. They always knew it was haunted, people wouldn't go down into the cellar on their own or go upstairs into the hotel they would always go in groups.

In 2007 Ellie started up Pillywiggins, after having a market stall for 8 years she decided to set up shop in The Dolphin selling crystals, skulls, witches kitchen items, everything spiritual including 16 handmade Ouija boards. Not long afterward the cellar became flooded where all the items were stored. Everything was damaged…. except the Ouija boards!

It makes you wonder how intelligent the spirits of The Dolphin are. They gave Ellie a false sense of security so that she would love the hotel with a passion before she saw the mischievous dark side. The underbelly of something not only playful, at times charming and intriguing but also a dark side that would become more apparent as time went by. A side that was desperate to have a voice, it was a time for the spirits to be heard.

About this time an imp which is classed as a demonic energy was caught on camera of the old CCTV in the bar of The Dolphin, you will find the photo at the back of the book. The original footage was sent to the Paranormal Science Team who came to the hotel and ran various experiments over the course of three days to see if the imp was manually put on there, to debunk, or declare that this case was truly paranormal. Ellie not being technical what so ever, was told the pixel was going in time so it was part of the CCTV and could not be explained? They didn't know what it was so the figure captured was classed as paranormal; the video has since gone viral and can be found on The Haunted Dolphin Hotel Facebook page. There have also been several orbs going in a directional route even changing in mid float and flashing, debunking the dust theory. One orb of light looks like a long dragon and snakes its way around the bar of the hotel. An Angel has also been captured coming up from a table and flying up to the ceiling, various tests have been carried out to try and debunk it as a reflection, but there is absolutely no explanation. These can also all be found with the full video of the angel on The L.I.G.H.T Paranormal Facebook page.

Ellie believes she was supposed to meet the man on the steps at St. Catherines that day, after being homeless for a couple of months sleeping rough on the beach. The touch of his hand on her head felt like red hot pokers and his words of, "Your life will change today!" Ellie remembers as clear as day even now, leading her to believe he was a medium or healer.

Third time lucky and Ellie's feet were firmly back in The Dolphin Hotel, "It's a funny old place," Ellie told me, "The Dolphin has a heartbeat all of its own and if you are not attuned to it, it spits you out!" Perhaps the hardship and experiences Ellie had gone through made her attuned to the energy and spirits of The Dolphin....

There were many times over the years before taking it over that Ellie would not go into The Dolphin because drugs were rife, with unsavoury characters and fights. Even after 20 years of struggle, up to her ears in debt, due to the law changing regarding smoking in the pubs, getting rid of trouble makers and the national chains charging next to nothing for drinks, her determination to keep the Dolly has never wavered. Ellie now just cannot compete; she is tied into the brewery and their charges. She refuses to give up the ghost, excuse the pun. The Dolphin is her home, it's her heart, and she defends it with a passion. The love Ellie has for the building and all who reside within its walls is unquestionable and I have to say in the very little time I have known Ellie and The Dolphin, I can understand why.

CHAPTER 4

The history of the building and the land that was

L ittlehampton is located on the coastal plain below the South Downs and at the mouth of the River Arun. It has always been a popular area to live, with evidence of human activity, burial sites, and coins of Constantine going back to Prehistoric, Bronze Age, and Roman times, respectfully. Littlehampton first appears in the written record as "Hantone", in the Doomsday Book of AD1086. A waxen thermograph map from Carentan in France from around AD1100 shows Littlehampton as a small fishing community at that time.

Bearing in mind that the Romans were a bit of a feisty bunch with raping and pillaging, torture and sacrifices, it is no wonder the land is a bit...busy spiritually, for want of a better word. Well, I did watch Spartacus... clues are there! After the Romans, the Saxons were not much better; there is also relic evidence of the Normans. There were various churches, monks, nuns, priests, Quakers, and Presbyterian that have all been documented in one way or another around the Littlehampton area through to medieval times, in that era, I would definitely emphasise the 'eval', even if it is spelled differently. From Saxon to Paganism, Littlehampton being a spiritual land before the churches were built. As far away from main cities and anything goes attitude Littlehampton may have been a haven of debauchery. With Arundel's dark history just up the river and the near location to Littlehampton, it would be no surprise for it to be caught up in the shenanigans of the dark ages.

In the year 1139 England was in the grips of a civil war. Both Stephen and Matilda claimed the throne. In that year the forces of Matilda came from France and landed in Littlehampton on her way to Arundel. I hardly think there was a discussion over tea and crumpets. Knowing our history the landing would have been more barbaric, perhaps a battlefield of blood.

Matilda was an indomitable woman! She was the daughter of King Henry I of England and was his sole legitimate child after the death of his son William. She was married first to Henry V of the Holy Roman Empire, and then when he died in 1125, her father Henry married her off again, this time to Geoffrey Plantagenet, Count of Anjou.

Matilda was nominated by her father as the heir to the throne of England, but in 1135 Stephen of Blois claimed that his uncle had changed his mind on his deathbed, recognising Stephen instead as his successor to the throne. The powerful English barons backed this claim. Matilda was incensed at this news and refused to accept this decision quietly.

Stephen did not have the ruthless temperament required to control the ensuing turmoil as civil war broke out when his dispute with Matilda became common knowledge. This period of civil war became known as 'The Anarchy' and lasted for 19 years.

Stephen was more popular than Matilda, as she was viewed by most of the people as a foreigner, Matilda was also found to have an unfortunate personality. She was proud and overbearing, arranging everything as she thought fit, according to her whim. How to gain friends and influence people.... not!

Matilda did not get the crown as she had hoped ...not because she was lacking in courage ...but more because she had an arrogant and haughty manner, and was heartily disliked, lovely!

Any battle, especially where deaths are involved leave residual, spiritual energy perhaps trapped in a continual replay on a time loop of the past.

1348 The Bubonic Plague is also known as the Black Death, this was not just Littlehampton's battle but also all of Sussex. This was often a fatal pandemic disease that is believed to have originated in Asia, swept across Europe, and eventually to England. In the summer of 1348, the first deaths in England were recorded. The earliest and nearest reported cases to Sussex were in Southampton in the neighbouring county of Hampshire. The disease was carried by the fleas on the rats that frequently infested ships holds. While the disease spread overland from Southampton, it undoubtedly also entered Sussex directly via its ports and inlets. The symptoms of the disease are a high fever, muscle cramps, and seizures, followed by the development of painful lymph gland swellings known as buboes. These were commonly found in the groin and sometimes in the armpits or neck, usually at the site of the initial infection. In the current day, Bubonic Plague can be successfully treated with antibiotics, but in the fourteenth century, before the discovery of antibiotics, death resulted in 50% to 90% of cases. All areas of Sussex were affected by the disease. The loss of life in some villages was so great that the villages were abandoned. The bodies were buried in plague pits... the children of The Dolphin tend to sing ring a ring a roses...Are they victims of such a diabolical illness stuck in the ever-revolving doorway to spirit who are too afraid to cross over?

The river Arun became a hive of activity with coastal trade up to Arundel and London with ships also going to the continent in the 16th and 17th centuries. The ships bringing many sailors and visitors in on the tide intensified the spread of the plague again in 1665. There had been smaller outbreaks over the years but this one was catastrophic. So intense was the outbreak that thousands of people died wiping out whole families in London and the surrounding areas.

In 1735 a new river mouth channel was cut and a wooden harbour erected at Littlehampton to establish the port opening. The river was diverted away from The Dolphin at this time but the old riverbed still floods today. In the late 18th century Littlehampton began to thrive as a seaside town, visitors came for bathing and were chiefly accommodated in the village at

The Dolphin Inn. The original Dolphin Inn, situated where the White Hart is today was owned by two brothers, they ended up having a bit of an argument. One of the brothers moved out and brought the land where the convenience and livery building was, he then decided to build his own hotel. Once it had been built he named it The Dolphin Inn, obviously to really p...cheese his brother off. For a while there was two Dolphin Inns, the brother living in the original Dolphin eventually changed it to The Swan, it has also been known as the White Heart and Cob & Pen. During the history of The Dolphin, there have been 3 major fires since it was first constructed, 1832 being the first, the last being 1928. There have since been many minor fires, always in room 3. How, is questionable!

As the town became full of hustle and bustle there were stocks for law and order, a poor house, a children's orphanage in the late 1800s, just down the road. Having seen Oliver Twist and the documented history, I can only imagine the hardship and treatment of the children in that environment. The care of these poor young souls was not top of the list in those times, hence, why so many children reside within the walls of The Dolphin. Perhaps at that time a beacon of light and spiritual energy in a dark world.

When you look at the colourful history including smugglers, not only at The Dolphin Hotel but also on the land where it sits, no wonder there is so much spiritual activity.

At the turn of the 19th century, there was an outbreak of diphtheria. The Dolphin's dank, dark, cold cellar was the obvious choice for the sick to stay to try and keep their temperatures down. Many of the poor souls were children, did they decide to stay rather than go with a body that could no longer sustain the spiritual energy of life?

In 1918, an influenza epidemic, known as the Spanish Flu, hit Littlehampton. The Dolphin became the go-to place to store the surplus decaying corpses due to the cold and damp conditions. Hundreds of bodies were stored along with the spirits attached to them, so intense was the disease that the local morgue could not cope with the volume.

The Second World War resulted in soldiers being killed, houses being bombed with fatalities. Was The Dolphin like a beacon of light to the poor lost souls? One spirit proved that indeed he found comfort in the walls of The Dolphin after his house was bombed. He was more concerned about finding his bike than the fact he had died. The Dolphin was again being used as an overspill for bodies during the war.

Just to recap, during the vast history of the surrounding land and the building, with supposedly scientific evidence that buildings and items hold on to energy if Einstein's theory is anything to go by; Einstein proved that all energy of the universe is constant and that it can neither be created nor destroyed... so what happens to the energy when we die if it cannot be destroyed? It must then according to Dr. Einstein, be transferred into another form of energy! Whether he had ghostly or spiritual apparitions, orbs, sensations, sounds, or a re-enactment of an event on a time loop in mind, resulting in the Stone Tape theory, well that's a different story! Then it is no wonder that The Dolphin Hotel is so active. As time goes forward in the 21st-century spirit are stuck in the time they lived, some not realising they are no longer living on the earth plane but existing in another dimension. At The Dolphin we work with the spirit, good and bad, to give them a voice to tell their tale and if they wish, help them to cross over back into the light, which is an energy force within itself.

CHAPTER 5

The rooms with a ghostly view

With an array of rooms to stay in they all have their unique spookiness. Due to the spiritual activity in rooms 1 and 2, they are rarely rented out as they are not for the faint-hearted. Feeling sick, pounding headache, tingling sensations in the legs, and feeling restricted around the throat, breathlessness, tight chest, clothes being pulled, and scratches often appearing, in both these rooms. Perhaps the negative energy flows from one room to another through the door that connects them. In fact, all the sensations can be felt all over the hotel!

Room 1 has a heavy, cold, oppressive air that draws people to the window. After the incident with the barmaid, if someone did jump out now they will land on the wooden gazebo instead. On a recent ghost hunt one of the guests who attended sat in this room on their own and felt the presence of Molly's spirit the good-time girl, unfortunately, her advances were often denied. To ease her pain she hung herself in the stables that used to be situated at the back of The Dolphin opposite rooms 1, 2, and 3.

One credible report of Molly's ghost came from an American serviceman in the mid-1990s. While relaxing at The Dolphin Hotel he was suddenly stunned to see the ghostly apparition of a woman walking across the floor in front of him. Further investigation indicated that Molly's apparition had indeed appeared over the old stable block, where she had met her tragic end and since the floor had been raised several times, it explained the man's odd report: he said that Molly appeared to be wading through water; her ghostly apparition was only visible from the waist up.

Room 2 is also oppressive and cold with a lady in white who is often seen walking through the walls and out of the window.

This was witnessed by a couple who had booked in for the week and paid in cash. On the first night, the gentleman came down to the bar at 10 pm wearing nothing but a towel! He was clearly shaken and explained that a woman had come through the door. After being told that he could lock the door from the inside he went on to explain that she had actually floated through the door and then out through the closed window. He asked if they could be moved which Ellie happily obliged and put them into room 6. When Ellie went up in the morning with their breakfast, she found they had gone and checked the CCTV discovering they had left at 4.30 am; they couldn't get out quick enough. Ellie tied to contact them by phone and email but they were never to be heard of again, not even for a refund! Their story was then published in the local newspaper which was printed in April 2005. It can be found under 'Newspaper Articles'.

The cupboard in room 2 is also very questionable, it is freezing! There is a portal entrance in the cupboard that goes up into the cupboard in room 3. It causes the EMF meter to go mad anytime it is anywhere near the door. Just to recap portals are like wormholes that come from another dimension onto the earth plane where spirit can come and go as they please, and EMF reads electric and magnetic fields which can be created by spirits. While I was on a tour of the hotel with Ellie, a priest, and a monk popped in but they definitely did not have saintly intentions on their mind. On the many ghost hunts held in the hotel, people are asked to stand inside, if they dare of course! Spirit are only too happy to oblige making themselves known by touching their face, hands, legs, in fact, any part of the body of the willing victims...I mean guest! It is a bit daunting seeing as they are in a freezing cold closet with the door shut and an entrance to the other side, which side is questionable. Whilst in room 2 conducting an EVP recording, this is a device to record spirits noises and voices, Ellie picked up the sound of a cow mooing. The Dolphin is nowhere near fields, a haunting sound playing on replay from the cows that used to pass by the window which was then a public right of way. Was it the last call for help on the way to the slaughterhouse by St. Catherines Field? Disembodied voices have also been recorded. A medium who's house backs on to the pub's garden and opposite room 2's portal, claims she sees spirits coming and going at all hours of the day! Making Piccadilly Circus look like the Mary Celeste!

In 2015 Christine Spry was booked into room 2 with her partner at The Dolphin Hotel for 4 nights to celebrate her 60th Birthday. After a wonderful evening, they decided to settle down for a quiet night with no idea how active and crazy it would turn out to be. Christine's mobile phone was pushed off the nightstand by an invisible force; they then felt the bed dip down as if someone was sitting on it and the coat hangers in the wardrobe started clanging together, not just moving but literally swinging around like someone had run their hand across them! Footsteps echoed not only around the room but outside the door and in the corridor with no one there. Bedraggled from a sleepless night they cut their visit short and left the next day. On hearing about a ghost hunt by the Most Haunted Experience she commented on her stay and confirmed the information with Ellie. This year to celebrate her 65th Birthday they are going camping...I wonder why!

Room 3 is hideous, a very strange room indeed! When Ellie first came to The Dolphin in 1988 the room was burnt out. Nowhere else in the hotel had any damage. The room was then redecorated. When Ellie returned in 1993 half the room was burnt out again! Was it a coincidence? When Ellie returned in the year 2000 the very same room was completely blackened, burnt-out yet again and this time because of being the owner Ellie had to pay for the repairs. The whole room has been burnt out 3 times; this is not including the major fires. Each time only the room smelt of burning no other part of the hotel was affected by the odour. In fact, the whole hotel has been burnt down 3 times over the years the last one in 1928, you can see in the photograph section how the hotel has changed since it was first built.

It had been reported that every time a fisherman was seen a fire followed...

In 2013 a very respectable lorry driver not known for tall tales was staying in room 3 for 6 weeks. He opened the door on his last night to find a full apparition of a fully dressed, old fashioned fisherman complete with sou'wester hat standing in the doorway. There used to be 3 fisherman cottages at the back of the hotel. Shocked, the driver looked away and when he looked back again the apparition had gone! Now just before this event and to set the scene; the bed was pushed up against the cupboard in room 3 so you would have to move the bed completely out of the way to open it. During the night, the lorry driver told Ellie that the bed had started shaking and vibrating; when he sat up and turned the light on to see what was happening he saw the cupboard wide open with the bed in the middle of the room! He was shocked as he told Ellie, "There was no way it could have opened, it was shut and I was in the bed when I went to sleep!" Perhaps in this case the fisherman may have been one of the victims that died in the many fires and was just coming to say hello or even goodbye as he was leaving the next day, this time without the matches. The smell of fire can still be smelt but only in this room.

On a recent ghost hunt with Penji the pendulum firmly in my hand, something was confirmed that both Ellie and I had been feeling, that the landlord actually jumped out of room 3's window because of the fatality of his injuries even though the pulling sensation towards guest is in room 1. Perhaps it is because the window in room 1 is more accessible so increases the chances of gathering another soul? If you look at the front cover photograph of the top window which is room 3 you can make out a shape at the window. This was just after we had left the room and locked it up with no one able to enter. Maybe the landlord was watching...

This room is also where Prudence first made contact and the

last place she was alive, a prostitute who met her untimely end to an overzealous punter; check out the famous and infamous spirit section in the book.

One of the reasons behind the dark oppressive air of room 3 has just recently come to light. Ellie and I used an Ouija board with K2's which pick up electromagnetic fields, using the different coloured lights spirit can manipulate them to communicate, spirit box for disembodies voices and other devices to connect with 'Jane' and the spirits of The Dolphin Hotel. If the spirits are to be believed this is Jane's story.

William worked doing odd jobs within The Dolphin Hotel in the mid-1700s, a sinister-looking character, smelly and un-kempt, mean as they come who would leer after the ladies, a loner who never married. Jane worked in the kitchen as a cook, a lovely woman only too happy to help, loved by everyone and very pretty. William was apparently her uncle and was very aware of how lovely she was and often loitered in the shadows watching her. Jane avoided him as she always felt uneasy in his company, never in the same room as him if she could avoid it and definitely, never alone because he accosted her at every opportunity. Many mediums picked up that perhaps Jane was pregnant after one too many attacks by William but Jane was too afraid to say because of his threatening behaviour and who would believe her. Women were seen as nothing more than mere objects, they were controlled, oppressed, downgraded, seen as second in importance, and just reproductive vessels full of petty emotions; women were there to do as they were told! One day when the hotel was busy and the staff was run off their feet, Jane took food orders up to the rooms, on one such trip William was loitering in the shadows watching. After Jane had delivered the food to room 7 she started to return to the kitchen but she never arrived. William was waiting on the landing out-side room 3, as soon as Jane came through the door he grabbed Jane and dragged her into the room that had been vacated earl-ier that morning. He chucked her down onto the bed and raped her again, full of rage from her constant rejection, his stalking obsession to own and take her after watching her for so long became his only purpose. He ravished her poor helpless body while holding her by the throat to keep her still, the weight of his body, and with the strength of a man possessed, William did not notice that she had taken her last breath, Jane's body now devoid of life. Is he or other energies at work that keeps starting so many unexplained fires, perhaps to burn away the residue memories of the hideous crimes committed in this room? There are still so many questions that need answering. I have tried to trace them back by census; however, the first census took place in 1801, 74 years of history before people were documented. The census, however, is another story! Now Jane's tale has been told perhaps she will find peace.

Room 4 has a very strange atmosphere, severe temperature fluctuations occur and a feeling of pressure in your head. In 2012 an ex-navy, policewoman and now a lawyer was conducting a ghost hunt in the room when she came running out screaming, She said that a very tall, dark man was standing next to her breathing deeply making her feel awful and scared the life out of her. A priest also stayed in this room in 2013, he came down the following morning and asked Ellie for a chair, he then came down again and asked for some sugar, on the third time he came down and asked if he could be moved. When Ellie asked him, "Why?" he responded by saying, "'there is an evil presence in my room and I don't like it!" He was obviously building up the courage to say something that is completely out of the norm to most people but not to the landlady of The Dolphin. He was of course promptly moved. At least he stayed!

While conducting ghost hunts in room 4 a child has been seen sitting on the bed, he has also been caught and photographed on a live feed. When guests enter the room, a woman has also been felt next to the boy omitting negative energy. Is this a governess watching over her ward or someone exploiting an orphan? When groups of people go into the room the other children follow. Lord Byron pops into this room now and then too.

In 1992 Patricia Reardon aged 17 stayed in room 4, at the time she had an overbearing and controlling boyfriend who was a bit too slap-happy with his fist and would often beat her. While living there she used to hear and sense things, one day when he was about to hurt her again, the closed door swung open with such a force it stopped him in his tracks. There was no one outside in the corridor, no other guests in the hotel at that time and the door had been firmly shut, perhaps the other victims of The Dolphin heard her cries and came to Patricia's aid? After the incident, she always felt safe in room 4, and because of her spiritual experience, she now has empathic abilities. The boyfriend... well after that incident he legged it and was never heard of again, a bully had met his unseen match!

Room 5, well here is the thing, even though it resides in one of the most haunted pubs in England this room is good to go for a full night spirit free sleep. Form an orderly queue as I feel this will be booked, constantly! Well at least until the spirits decide to pop in with a bedtime story...

Room 6, however, is a completely different story, especially if you're after a little slap and tickle but be warned before you rush to book the room, it might not be what you were hoping for. At least 50 men from all backgrounds have stayed in this room over the 20 years Ellie has been landlady. At least 20 of them had asked Ellie if a woman was staying at the hotel that had access to the room. When asked why, they said rather sheepishly I might add that they felt their genitals were being played with. Well, they were the only ones who dared to speak up; the others perhaps thought it was an added bonus! The downside to that is it's just down the corridor from room 4 where the priest stayed and felt the evil presence. As we know, evil can be demonic and under that title are incubus and succubus evil entities that disguise themselves as wanderlust energies:

Incubus and their sidekick Succubus are thought to be demons that have sexual relations with women and men, respectively, mostly while they are sleeping or in a compromised state. It has also been known to happen when the person is wide awake. It is thought by some that the incubus and succubus are the same entity simply switching backward and forwards from male to female, while others believe they are two entities entirely. However, Demons do not possess a single-sex, the same as spirit, when we die we tend to reincarnate back on to the earth plane as other life forms including men, women, and animals, no wonder some people don't know whether they are coming or going! When spirit shows themselves it is as they were in their last incarnation and how we would remember loved ones. Variations of the incubus and succubus can be found in folklore around the world, from historical to biblical mythology. No smoke without fire is what I say, especially with the numerous amounts of mediums, TV programmes and paranormal investigators also picking up on demonic energies... Just putting it out there...

Of course in between these rooms are long, dark corridors, stairways, and a fire escape all of which do not escape the odd visitation or 20....a day!

The staircase that leads up from the bar into the hotel is an active place for a sing-song. On my first tour around all I could hear was 'What becomes of the drunken sailor?' As I stood at the top of the stairs, visions of staggering sailors who had come in on the tide and booked a room for the night trying to climb the stairs, one it seemed lost his footing and broke his neck. There are newspaper clippings of questionable sailors ending up behind bars for naughty behaviour, including theft, death by brawling, along with smuggling which I will go into later in chapter 8.

At the top of the stairs is a glass fire door. One unsuspecting guest was climbing the stairs to be greeted by a man dressed in a 1600's cavalier uniform looking at him through the door, he then simply faded away. On a live ghost hunt, two cavaliers were also picked up in the back cellar by Steve Jennings from Stabbed in the Back Paranormal. He had no prior knowledge of the ghostly visitation.

Once you go through the fire door you reach the landing into the hotel section. Turning right there is an outside fire door that leads on to a fire escape which is not just used by the living. Children run up and down looking into the bedroom windows as they pass. On several occasions, there is an elegant lady who has her hair done up in a loose bun, high necked white blouse and long, Victorian-styled light coloured skirt. This is the lady in white who can be seen floating across the iron walkway.

Turning away from the fire escape a bathroom is in front of you and rooms 1 and 2 are on the right. Outside the room is a single flight of stairs which leads up through a door to a landing where room 3 is situated. On the stairs, you can often hear a ball bouncing, laughter of children and orbs, hundreds of them! As you carry on up the stairs the door creaks at the top giving full sound effects of a haunted hotel worthy of any horror movie, that in itself is enough to make the hairs go up on the back of your neck and make you look behind you.

On opening the next fire door it leads you to a long, dark, cold corridor that goes past all the rooms and ultimately leads to room 7, but that deserves a chapter all of its own. Once through the door, you stand on a landing outside room 3 where one of the cooks from years gone by normally stands. Wearing an old fashioned cooks dress and matching hat, she certainly was not starved if her robust and voluptuous figure is anything to go by, even in death. I see her every time I go to this section of the hotel and she always looks pleased to see me, perhaps because she knows I can see her. She has come through on my Angel table as I like to call it and has given me the initials E.J which stands for Elizabeth Jane Holliss, the landlord Robert Holliss's wife.

There is another bathroom on this level before going through the other fire door. On the other side are even more orbs, the corridor it leads on to runs along the length of the private residence below, this is where Ellie and her partner could hear running and the child's laughter. Since then a child crying has also been heard within the cavities. A child buried within the walls? Anything is possible in the foundations of THIS hotel! It was while I was on my tour with Ellie, turning right we stopped at a window that cannot be seen from the front of the hotel due to the frontage. As Ellie reach out and explained the structure of the hotel her hand was struck from an unseen force causing Ellie to jump back and grab her hand. Maybe something was getting just a little too touchy about the things we were unveiling on our travels.

Carrying along the corridor past the rooms, there is one doorway that appears to be boarded up but for some reason, I could not seem to go past it, my pendulum was going mad. A young woman was shown to me, she was lying on the bed, her clothing which looked from the era of the early 1800s was in disarray and her body was a mass of lacerations. She was saying, "Help me" over and over again. At this point, Ellie's ghost hunting equipment Paratek showed 'help me!' Still hearing her screaming and not be able to go past this doorway was a sign to me that this unfortunate soul wished to be crossed over and I was only too happy to help. Many souls that reside within the walls of The Dolphin are trapped by their fear, so continually stay within the walls, some do ask to be crossed over and I willingly oblige.

Walking around The Dolphin, there is a creepy air of foreboding, the cloud of cold breath in front of you as the temperature drops is also a giveaway to the feelings of being watched and followed. Footsteps echo around you, balls bouncing along the corridor, the sound of skipping, children giggling, whispering, and muffled conversations. Banging, rattling, knocking on windows from the outside even though it is 3 stories up, all very strange indeed. A regular guest at The Dolphin has also experienced being shoved into the walls of the corridors or was it a few too many in the bar? Perhaps you need to pop along to make your own mind up if you dare...

CHAPTER 6

*Room 7 boys and girls
should go to heaven*

This used to be the old nursery and part of the original building. Ellie would let this room out which had bunk, double and single beds inside at one time or another, but guests felt uneasy. A couple that stayed in there long term experienced strange things happening, including leaving a curry in its take-away containers on the side while they had a nap, only to wake up and find all of it had disappeared! They tried to blame the cat who lived 3 floors down in the private residence, unless it was a spider cat there was no way it could of gone though all the fire doors, corridors and mastered a locked door to eat it. At that point there was no one else staying in the hotel. Vindaloooo-ooohhhh anyone!

A magazine journalist tried to stay in room 7 all night for her story; she lasted 2 hours and then fled. The article that she wrote can be found on the Facebook page.

After several refunds because of the oppressive atmosphere Ellie stopped renting it out to passing guests. They would continually hear noises, banging, lights flashing, coins and marbles being thrown, shuffling in the old inbuilt cupboard, having scratches and found huge spiders that were not found in any other part of the hotel, which is a bit discouraging and not conducive of a good night's sleep. A wayward tarantula spreading his legs very wide indeed with his family and moved in! They would have mood swings including depressive thoughts, the people not the spiders... and just generally a feeling of being out of sorts. At this point Ellie decided not to rent it out and changed it back to a nursery to use on ghost hunts with trigger objects. Until a group of five ladies stayed the night for charity, the original newspaper clip can be found in the photograph section. The ladies were members of the Littlehampton Carnival Association who spent the night on a sponsored scare-a-thon. Before bedding down the ladies went on a quick tour of the pub where they heard gunshots and had stones thrown at them by playful spirits in the front cellar. Once they had settled the fear was so great and overwhelming they nearly made a bolt for the door, the thought that it was for charity made them stay. They could hear a sound like marbles were being rolled across the ceiling, three of the ladies saw a little girl with pigtails in her hair wearing white old fashioned clothes, was this little Dolly? Thankfully they all emerged the next morning to tell the tale with a new found respect for spirit and open to many possibilities.

On the beginning of the program of Help! My House Is Haunted one of the camera crew Andy, went up to room 7. As he was positioning the cameras, the lights flashed on and off. Never have I seen anyone move so fast out of there and running down the corridor like his life depended on it; take it his not coming back for a holiday any time soon then! The event was seen on the programme, what you didn't see was Ellie taking Barri Ghai back up to the room and showing him that the light that came on did not actually work. Saves on electric bills I suppose.....

On one of the first ghost hunts a strong female presence was felt, she was caught on camera entering room 7 which you will find in the photograph section. As she comes through the wall it's as if she is coming from another room except there is not one there. Perhaps she had a room in different quarters before the fires happened and that is the path she took in life to be repeated on replay, for eternity. The governess/nanny, as she is known had one particular charge that was a disfigured, disable child; Mark Green came face to face with his spiritual apparition while exploring the secret cupboard in room 7. In a day an age when any disabilities were frowned upon it is quite possible that some poor soul was hidden away in the many hidey holes within The Dolphin Hotel. He would have been classed as an embarrassment to the family so when there were guests or visitors he was hidden away. Any births of such were not registered due to the shame it would bring to the family. Thank goodness times have changed and everyone is equal. The boy is picked up every now and then but the nanny always makes her presence felt, just recently on a live ghost hunt the energies were picked up by many mediums as they watched. When we are conducting ghost hunts she often comes in to offer her protection from the many negative energies that show up every now and then. When alive the nanny looked after the children, in death dedicated to her profession she continues to watch over their souls as they seem forever trapped in room 7 and The Dolphin Hotel.

When you walk into the room you will see an old wooden rocking horse, a high chair, a cot and old toy pram with various dolls inside, a settee and comfy chair, a dolls house, oh and a small Ouija table. Perhaps those items do not seem that intimidating... well except the Ouija table. However, each item is a trigger object for the young spirit children that play in this room and are all authentic.

The rocking horse is an antique with a history within itself. Over a hundred years old it was found in the attic of room 7, when Ellie moved in. It has a will of its own so it may seem, every so often it will move as if it is being ridden by an invisible force, starting slowly building up to a gallop and then stops dead. There is nothing unusual about that one then! On a live feed the rocking horse has had touch sensitive flashing balls placed on top. The horse started slightly rocking and the balls started flashing, the SLS camera showed two stick children standing besides it. A screen shot of the SLS figures can be found in the photograph section. The live feed can be found on The Haunted Dolphin Hotel and The L.I.G.H.T Paranormal Facebook page.

There are two high chairs, one recently found in an attic space above the top bathroom, and the other was found in the loft space above room 7, both dating back to well over a hundred and fifty years old. A ghostly little boy can be seen sitting in one of the chairs kicking his arms and legs, laughing, snap shot to happier times in the past, perhaps. He wears a Victorian, blue baby suit and holds a wooden rattle, if you listen carefully you can hear the noise it makes, a slight jingling in the quiet, night air.

The old Victorian child's toy pram found in the attic as well, also has an energy force all of its own. Filled with various dolls, when a flashing cat ball is placed inside the children communicate by making it flash in answer to questions asked. There is nothing like passing the time away sitting in the dark watching a flashing light show with no one nearby, except for the unseen spirits of the dead children who still want to play mummies and daddies.

The settee and chair seem innocent enough or are they? People who sit on them during ghost hunts can feel pressure, cold spots and tickling on their bare legs, pulling on clothes, feeling as if something is near to their faces. All these signs perhaps are of children wanting to be played with or comforted, trying to let people know they are still there wanting to be acknowledged and loved. A guest at a ghost hunt had what felt like a stick smacked across his legs, he was left with red marks over both, maybe they thought he was being naughty...

The cot dates back to Georgian times, perhaps a family heirloom passed down through the generations which also ended up in the attic of The Dolphin. When one in three children died of one illness or another at that time including; measles, mumps, diphtheria, scarlet fever, rubella, dysentery, cholera, influenza, small pox and T.B to name but a few. All of which can be treated today which is a little too late for The Dolphin's children. It is hardly surprising that when an Empath stands too close to the cot, a tightness of the chest and difficulty breathing can be felt. A little baby boy often appears lying in the cot listless, was he at the mercy of some unsuspecting adult who had coughed perhaps just a little too closely one too many times? His little soul has long since departed but the residual energy remains trapped within the wooden confinement of the cot with just his whimpering sound left, a long since forgotten death playing on a memory loop perhaps...Flashing balls also go off in the cot when place inside.

The various dolls that line the cot have all been donated at one time or another to Ellie because each has their own story to tell, they just have not told it yet. The attachments are apparent as the eyes of the dolls seem to follow you as you walk around the room. Attachments can happen not just to humans but also to objects, many spirits who pass with a belief that there is no life after death find themselves floating around and can attach themselves to various items. Dolls in particular are a favourite because of their human form perhaps, along with furniture, jewellery, ornaments and believe it or not clothes! If you don't fancy any uninvited quests coming into your house I would suggest saging, also known as smudging, by burning the sage while fanning the smoke over the items and reciting the Lord's Prayer, if in doubt Google it. Laughter, giggling and whispering tends to come from the little cot and pram. One bald headed baby doll appeared out of nowhere and two had to be removed, here are their tales;

Susie: She has been moved to the other high chair which was recently found in a second loft. Looking like an innocent tiny tears doll of the 50's you would think this would be a fabulous doll to have. Fast forward 40 years and nothing can be further from the truth, bearing in mind the infamous stories behind Robert Doll, Annabelle, Harold, Mandy and Peggy each were found to have attachments and be dolls possessed, worth a Google. Susie was used on a live feed by Ellie and Mark Green it is worth having a look at it in The Haunted Dolphin Hotel Facebook page. The story behind Susie is that she was given to Ellie as a child from a woman who classed herself as a witch. Now we know they come in different guises from the herb loving white, pagan witch, who is full of love and light. Then of course the dodgy Hansel and Gretel kind of witch who you avoid at all costs! From the way Susie behaved I can honestly say the woman needed her credentials examined! Anyway, Ellie's mum worked as a cleaner and a client had given her Susie which she gave to Ellie when she was 3 years of age. Ellie didn't really like the doll without knowing why, so she put her away in the cupboard. Over the years she kept finding Susie in different parts of her room, thinking her mum, who had a wicked sense of humour, was finding her in the cupboard and was taking her out as a joke. Things would go missing only to turn up a few days later without any explanation. Things in her room would be pushed off the shelf and broken, she thought it was the cat but her room was out of bounds because of allergies. It wasn't until her teenage years when her then girlfriend was up in her room, that they could hear a clicking sound. This same sound Ellie had heard numerous times over the years and because she could never find out where it came from just dismissed it. However, it seemed louder than usual so together they tracked down the sound to Susie in the cupboard. When they got her out they could hear the noise coming from inside her so shook the doll and a death watch beetle fell out through a hole it had chewed in Susie's back. By now, Ellie was so spooked by the beetle that seemed to have been alive for so many years, that she went down and asked her mum about Susie and where she had came from. "Who is Susie?" Ellie's mum asked, and when Ellie reminded her, she replied that she had not seen the doll in years since she gave it to Ellie! Shocked, Ellie asked her where she got it from. Ellie's mum explained that she cleaned for a bit of an eccentric woman who had given her the doll. Looking mortified Ellie realised it was the same woman who would scare kids, she would swear at the children, saying incarnations and spells at them, telling them that she was a witch and would put a curse on them for walking past her house. There was no other way to get to school so they had to go past her home and she would run to her gate shouting and screaming. Given to her in 1970 Susie had been living with Ellie all that time, there was no other explanation, Susie had a mind of her own. Ellie locked her away in a sealed box, and when she left home, her mother made sure she took it with her. Was Susie responsible for Ellie's bad luck in life? Ellie moved out and led her life with Susie not far away, until she moved into The Dolphin, she was left in a box in a cupboard and has only just been rediscovered when Ellie was sorting one of the rooms out. Recently Ellie and Mark did a live feed with Mark using UV light to entice the attachment in Suzie to show itself by doing transfiguration. Yeah, I know right.... who in the hell would say yes! Only a ghost hunter investigating of course! Luckily I am just a face on the screen as I was not in the room but joined in on the live feed, which means on a video call. The UV is used by ghost hunters for the spirit to show their face under the light on a willing subjects face... ok, maybe not such a willing subject in this case with Mark. Interesting viewing, you can find it on The Haunted Dolphin Hotel Facebook page under Suzie. For those that haven't got it, in brief, basically the spirit use ectoplasm under the UV coloured lights to manipulate the features on your face to resemble the spirit who is trying to communicate. Marks face ended up looking frightening, his eyes, nose and mouth completely changing with horns seeming to be forming out of his cheeks and head. Photographs can be found in the transfiguration section. At this point both myself and Ellie where yelling at Mark to come back and believe me he looked pretty out of it. The energy was dark, sinister and negative and attacked Marks voice box. I did warn him it would to be fair... it took a good few minutes for him to come round. At one point Ellie felt threatened by this entity that had attached itself to Mark and did not recognise it as being him. The energy stepped away but was still loitering in the room in no hurry to go back into Susie.

The resident spirits were out of sorts because of the darkness of this entity. He obviously hadn't had enough of a scare because Mark and Ellie went up into the attic above room 7; no one had been up there in over 19 years, since they found the nursery furniture. They were met by an energy force which showed itself as a bright, solid light that moved towards Mark, stopped, moved on, and then came back again! Photograph stills can be found under 'Orbs and light anomalies.' Deeply dark, and the most disturbing thing of all looking at the video of the attic as a medium, and seen by others on the live feed, all we could see was rows of spirit children. One little boy can be seen sitting on the floor hugging his legs which can be found in the 'Fabulously spooky' section, while he was being watched over by this dark entity. A soldier complete with handle bar moustache and a lady in a long, white dress were also in the attic, were they trying to protect the children from this dark energy?

Two days later I felt the need to ring Mark and on a video chat could instantly see the entity in his aura. Once I had left the live feed it stepped back in. I see people's auras, the life force around your body. I can see the colours, also I can tell if people have attachments, and there, as bold as brass, was this nasty sucker! I have many guides and work with Angels, I would not be able to say all the information I give at demonstration and in church services and readings without them. They are also my protectors which allows me to cross over or get rid of nasty spirits without the fear of attachments. Mark, by this point was coughing, finding it difficult to breathe and speak, he also felt exhausted and just looked like crap. Talking to the spirit, he didn't want to return to the spirit realm because of the evil he had done on the earth plane so I gave him the option to return from whence he came, believing him to be attached to Suzie, the very next day. The more I conversed with this energy, I found he had not actually come from Susie, her attachment had been over shadowed by this malevolent spirit, the energy force in the attic had come from Binstead wood.

Mark and Ellie had gone to Binstead Wood in Sussex on a ghost hunt. Due to being in the New Forest I was on a live feed so could see where they were going and what spirits were about. Binstead wood is known for its dark energies, signs of alleged Satan worship, from carcases of animal remains and general signs of quite frankly dodgy behaviour. Going into the woods both Mark and Ellie had this sense of being watched and followed, which I confirmed with the running commentary of spirits that I could see, including the dark male energy. I told them that they needed to get out of there pronto! Most people bring back a bluebell or two, maybe a gnarled piece of wood, no not Ellie and Mark, they brought back Slender/Shadow man as we called him. He attached himself to Mark as he too is empathic. Mark became very sick and out of sorts around the time he took part in the transfiguration with Ellie, and was becoming increasingly ill. As I was still in the New Forest I had not seen Mark other than through the video feed, spirits can be dodgy little devils when they want to be and can hide in plain sight. If you are in the room they are far easier to detect. After seeing Mark was not himself on the video call, I found the dark energy from Binstead was sitting in his aura. He was told in no uncertain terms that he needed to leave Mark even if it meant going back into The Dolphin. Slender man, after being threatened with being crossed over, went and took up residence in room 7 with Susie's attachment, the battle for power began.

Now the unnerving part is a tall, slim, dark suited man always seems to be there when people visit on ghost hunts and on the live feeds. He likes women to be women and dress accordingly; he does not like women in trousers. He took a dislike to one of the female barmaids; any flash of cleavage would result in him scratching her. The children seem to fear him and tend to be more subdued when he is near. When there are ghost hunts, he likes to follow and watch the guests every move, projecting negativity and he has the ability to turn people against each other. He likes to think he owns the place but he needs to form a queue as William and Fredrick are way ahead of him, but let me assure you there is only one person in charge and that is Ellie! Susie's attachment faded into the shadows temporarily, with the dark, oppressive energy of Slender man taking over and being constantly picked up in live feeds.

By Christmas 2019 Slender man just had to go, other guests were getting scratched, the feeling in room 7 was becoming very uneasy and the children's energies were changing from playful to fearful. Overwhelming feelings of sadness, anxiety and general discomfort would be felt in this room. Now you may be thinking, REALLY! But it's haunted! Let me explain there are different types of Casper's, from going on countless ghost hunts in The Dolphin you get to know the energies and what the spirits look like. When Slender man came in it drastically changed. Susie's attachment was getting the blame, even as menacing as it could be, it was nowhere near as bad as Slender man.

On the 16th of December 2019 seven of us from the development circle went up to room 7 and banished Slender man from The Dolphin. How we did it is in chapter 7. Believe me he did not want to go, the whole room shook, there was loud bangs, the floor vibrated, for over an hour we stood up to Slender man, then all of a sudden, silence..... Seven of us witnessed what happened in that room, even now, when we speak about it, it gives us goose bumps!

Susie's attachment now comes forward, apprehensively, maybe from what he witnessed with Slender man, but still likes to mess with Mark and any other guest who dares to do transfiguration in the vicinity of Susie. A dark, overbearing energy who will play with your emotions, on Slender mans level? We are not quite sure as he is still wary but is a force to be reckoned with when you're strolling around the corridors on your own. Susie was even locked in a trunk complete with the attachment or so we thought, and put up in the loft for all to see on The Haunted Dolphin Facebook page live feed but he still found his way out and lurks in the shadows. Susie was taken out again hoping he would return to her and stay put but that remains to be seen. Infamous bad boy of The Dolphin, William also has learnt from the experience with Slender man and is certainly dubious, and as long as the spirits are respectful and still wish to stay they can remain... If they cause harm... well then that is a different story.

Demon Doll: No other name for it! Ellie originally brought it for Halloween because when you switch it on it would make a wooooo sound. However, in between Halloween it would sit in room 7, but due to its eerie looking face and the negative emotions people would feel every time they looked at it, Ellie hid it in the cellar... Oh and of course the fact it liked to make the wooooo sound when it was switched off, with no batteries inside! When Help! My House Is Haunted came to film the TV show at The Dolphin, they found the once hidden doll sitting on a pile of boxes, in a small room at the bottom of the stairs leading to the cellar, perhaps waiting to be found. The team confirmed it had a demonic presence attached to it as seen in the programme. Zac Baggins from Ghost Adventures and the producer of Help! My House Is Haunted heard about it and wanted to put it in his haunted museum in Las Vegas. Ellie, only too happy to get rid of it pronto and get a handsome fee, put the doll in a brown box and sealed it with thick, brown, postal tape to secure it and left it in the cellar awaiting instructions. Barri Ghai came back in January following the recording of the episode for the doll. Ellie went down to get the box with another member of her paranormal investigation team Mark Green, only to find that the box seemed very light. When they opened it they found the box empty! The box had no signs of the tape being taken off or sealed again. Mark and Ellie being investigators tried to debunk anything that is even remotely iffy that makes hauntings questionable, they couldn't understand what had happened to it. Both were stumped as they were together when they sealed it and together when they opened it. Perhaps old Demon doll wanted her own vacation and it wasn't going to be stuck in a glass case in any museum, bless! So where is it!?

The Dolls house is another fascinating antique full of history. This was given to Ellie by her late Mother who sadly passed in February 2020, aged 94. It had been handed down through the generations of her family and is well over 150 years old. There are various pieces of furniture which will attract the smallest of child, living and of course the dead. Whenever Ellie goes into the room which is left locked, only Ellie has the keys, the furniture has been moved around and turned upside down in different rooms of the doll's house. This has happened on the live feeds on a ghost hunts with no chance of anyone being able to do it. A game that is spine tingling to say the least, even more so when you cannot see your gaming opponent. Just recently while I was on a ghost hunt with Southern Paranormal Team, a small rocking horse was chucked out of the doll's house with such great force, it landed just short of the middle of the room where a group of us were standing and sitting including Theresa Hawkins from my psychic development circle.

When you walk into room 7 the children's energy is apparent. Many a medium have seen the children playing and skipping especially as they skip in a circle, as previously mentioned, singing Ring a ring a roses.... we all fall down. The song was about the plague; A ring a ring a roses being the rash on the skin, a pocket full of posies, the herbs to keep the plague at bay, A-tishoo, A-tishoo, the symptom, we all fall down, dead! Now you are probably wondering why a hotel built in 1735, has got children from the plague in 1348 & 1665. Well, if you didn't read chapter 4 with boring history here's a recap. In 1348 and 1665 an epidemic of the Bubonic Plague hit Sussex including Littlehampton, before making its way to London. As a result there was a plague pit where thousands of bodies were put into it, somewhere perhaps in Littlehampton. With the history of the land and The Dolphin Hotel being a hub of spiritual energy and a red portal drawing spirit energies from all over the place, plus the level of children that reside at The Dolphin which has increased over time, perhaps they feel safety in numbers. Miraculously, even after all the fires, room 7 remains intact, I wonder why, the children protecting it maybe?

When Ellie and I were walking around The Dolphin in preparation of writing this book, I was recording with Ellie doing a live feed. As I was talking I could feel someone trying to push or kick my knee and actually said this on the video. At the same time Ellie captured an orb coming out of, you guessed it, my knee!

The Ouija table, well that has given a wealth of information from the children and the spirits that reside within the room. William and Fredrick often use it to communicate, William just to make the glass go round and round while protesting his innocence and Fredrick... well he grunts, groans, growls and rolls barrels, he is a spirit of few words. The children love to talk through the table telling their ages, how they died, their life in general, in fact they are playful, funny and charming, at times they can be afraid of the ever changing spirits within The Dolphin, the most famous spirit child of all is Little Dolly,......she commands a chapter all of her own.

CHAPTER 7

The beating heart of The Dolphin:

The Function Room & Psychic Circle

Walking through the door into this large ornate room with the original grand chandeliers, there is a buzz of energy and anticipation within the air. They say buildings and objects hold on to the energies and memories of the past, I can understand why. Situated on the second floor at the top of the stairs on the left, this room throbs with a heartbeat all of its own. When Ellie moved into The Dolphin there was a huge Ouija written on the wall. Even though it has now been painted over, it will always be etched into the heart of The Dolphin, it was introduced long before Ellie took over. It is not surprising really when the Victorian era was all about mediums, séances, Ouija, and talking to the dead. Many of them were drawn to the notion that the living could talk to the spirits who had passed to another realm.

Even now, as you stand at the door looking in you can imagine a large, round table with an array of the well to do who would flock to the seaside, engaging with communicating with their loved ones who had passed. It was as popular as a mobile phone is today if you don't have one you are so last year!

Sitting in all their finery, expensive bustle dresses, and morning suits while Mystic Madame 'Sheshe' looked mysterious dressed in black, with thick, dark eye makeup and enough bangles and rings to create a goblet or 2. Thank goodness fashions changed!

Prominent Victorians such as Sir Arthur Conan Doyle, Sir William F. Barrett, Harry Price, enthusiast Pierre Curie, and even Marie Currie, all dabbled in spirituality and life after death. Apparently, Mary Todd Lincoln held séances at the Whitehouse after losing her son, which her husband Abraham Lincoln often attended. Even Charles Dickens was a member of the Ghost Club and his world-renowned story of 'A Christmas Carol' with Scrooge, Marley, and the ghost of Christmas past, present, and future; show his interest in the afterlife. Queen Victoria also displayed an interest and willingness to believe that spirits of the dead could communicate. On more than one occasion Victoria held séances to communicate with Prince Albert receiving messages by using mediums who acted as intermediaries, hence why séances were conducted in parlours, studios, in fact anywhere at all with enough space to allow the hopeful to connect with their loved ones. I mean what else were they supposed to do there was no internet or TV, believe it or not!

During the nineteenth century, mortality was rife especially in children, one's full life span was questionable and because of this, the Victorians had many rituals to overcome grieve. With such a fruitful market, charlatans crept out of the sewer exploiting vulnerable people with false communication. It is no wonder that spiritualism came under the magnifying glass and became debatable. A few bad eggs and the whole hen house gets slaughtered!

Spiritualism began in America in 1848, sisters Kate, Margaret, and Leah Fox claimed to communicate with a spirit that was supposedly in their home using knocks on wood. Eventually, they established themselves as mediums conducting public demonstrations and séances. However, forty years later Margaret Fox developed a conscience and published a confession in the New York World that the rapping's supposedly used by the dead to communicate during séances, was in fact made by the sisters themselves using their fingers and feet. Really! Way to go girls! No wonder it is hard for legitimate mediums to be taken seriously!

So baring in mind the history of the land, the spiritual movement, and the Victorians' passion for everything spiritual, it is no wonder The Dolphin Hotel has more spirits than a brewery. They had a taste for communication with legitimate mediums; the portal was well and truly open. Why wouldn't they be able to manipulate a flood in the cellar and protect the Ouija boards so they could be used once again? After all, they are more than capable of showing us signs that the universe and spirit are watching.

The function room used to be a dining room, however, on two occasions it has been rented out to long term clients as a hotel room, both of which had a ghostly experience. Drag queen and ex-Mayor Billy Blanchard was getting ready to go out, whilst doing his make up in the mirror he saw the spirit of a woman coming up behind him who then suddenly disappeared. An ex-employee called Melanie Hunt also stayed in this room after asking to be moved out of room 7 for obvious reasons and theft of her curry, the grass is not always greener! While getting ready in front of the same mirror, the spirit woman duly appeared behind her but when she turned around she had gone. When Melanie described her to Ellie she matched the description as told to her by Billy, and where the mirror has now been relocated in the corridors that lead to room 7, she is often seen floating about. Ellie has also seen a young boy in rags crouched down under the table; there is a hint of soot when he appears, perhaps the bones inside the chimney belong to him. There is CCTV in this room so many unexplained moving shadows, shapes, and orbs appear. Mirrors are a wonderful tool for scrying; as you look into the mirror you ask spirit to show themselves using your face to do transfiguration. Just to recap that means ecto-plasm created from the spiritual energy moulds the face to take on the features of the spirit person, simple. The ectoplasm can also be used to take over the voice box so the spirit can speak through the host, who hasn't seen the movie Ghost? It is believed that mirrors are a portal to other realms. Just look at Snow White's stepmother, except hers was dark, very dark, who was a bit overzealous with the truth. You will find some more transfiguration and scrying in the photographs on The Haunted Dolphin Hotel and The L.I.G.H.T Facebook page.

Normally a portal tends to have one entrance but in The Dolphin's case, it has several, one of them being in the function room on the far left-hand corner as you face into the room. What do you do with a room with a portal in it? You start a psychic circle of course! I help people to develop their spiritual gifts. We all have the ability, it is like anything, you need to nurture your spirituality, learn to open up to spirit, to develop and grow. This is an awareness and a development of mediumship, clairvoyant; clear seeing, clairaudience; clear hearing, clairsentience; clear feeling, clairalience; clear smelling, clairgustance; clear tasting, claircognizance: clear knowing, by using all the senses and sitting with like-minded people who have always felt there is something more to life than meets the eye. Through meditation, it opens up our third eye, intuition, and sense of knowing through esp. (extra sensual perception). The abilities and senses become more heightened as you practice. Spiritual healers use their abilities by projecting them to help heal others. Their hands can burn and tingle, lightworkers all have the ability to do this, but it is where their strength lies that gives them their direction on which path to follow. So if you put a group of people who are interested in all things spooky and spiritual and place them in the middle of a spiritually active ghostly hub, expect the best to happen.

Since starting the psychic circle the activity has increased, in a more positive way than negative. I only work with love, light, and positivity; I have guides and work with angelic celestial light. No, I don't need a straight jacket thank you very much, and no one is coming to take me away just yet. The proof is in the evidence I give in church services, readings, and demonstrations, it has got to come from somewhere.

Through meditation and clearing your mind of every day emotional baggage that really does not serve you well, you can open your third eye to enhance the communication with spirit. This has taken a lifetime to perfect so it's not a 5-minute thing, commitment is essential as you are always learning. Teaching like-minded people is greatly rewarding to see their abilities develop. Now here's the thing, because of the spiritual energy that flows through The Dolphin, the people that attend the circles, well their abilities have just soared. What would normally take a person a few months to open up to, they have excelled in a matter of weeks by visualising, hearing and giving messages to others within the group, animals also come along with family members that have passed. When we work we are not alone, the children come in and play, pulling hair and clothes, tickling bare skin, skipping around as we meditate, and sitting against our legs, especially little Dolly. William looks on with a watchful eye; in fact, all the spirits of The Dolphin make an appearance at some point or another. I feel they love these sessions as it means they are not forgotten. They are part of our spiritual paranormal family and are just as intrigued about us as we are of them. We have also had spirits that have passed recently and lost their way through the confusion, they see the light of the portal emitting from the hotel which turns golden when we work because of the protection that surrounds us. I must stress, any work with spirits is done with strict opening and closing ceremonies, using crystals and other forms of protection that the group has learned before working with spirit. Any spirits are free to go to the light if they choose to and with the whole group's support we ensure they reach the spirit realm safely. The only time darkness comes is when we turn off the light at the end of the day, and then the dark energies of The Dolphin are free to roam the rooms and corridors once again.

Of course, we have the mischievous spirits that come in to try to disrupt the meditation by making it feel like the person is wearing earphones or a diving helmet, so they cannot hear me. This was experienced by Sandy at the start of the episode on

Help! My House Is Haunted featuring The Dolphin Hotel, not the circle but the helmet sensation. Worth watching even if it has been questionable especially regarding William and the holier than thou attitude he tried to portray. Once you tell your spirit guides to take it away they move the spirit off pronto. A gracious spirit will never encroach on your energies unless invited to do so. Much to the grumbling and moaning noises of the disgruntled spirits as their fun has been spoilt. The other sensation you can feel is the cobweb effect around your face, believe me, I would know if a spider even tiptoed past the door let alone came into the room, not that I am afraid of them or anything......I'm working on it!

After mediation, the room becomes very crowded with the spirits eager to give messages. The energy is electric, many different noises and sensations can be felt. We work with all our senses, also using photos, Angel boards, and objects for psychometry; where we read the energy and imprint left on an item by loved ones. The group learns about past life regression, spiritual art, inspirational writing, mediumship skills, the 7 principles of spiritualism, in fact, an array of things far too many to mention. Anyone looking to join development circles please make sure it is from a respectable, experienced medium that has been referred preferably by a spiritualist church. Ensure protection is explained, if they do not do this, or say it is not important, find one who understands the importance of self-protection. At the end of the day any Tom, Dick, or serial killer could pop in as an orb of energy into your aura, you need to be protected..... Just saying!

When the psychic circle is underway the activity increases, under the ever-watchful eye of the CCTV it films flashing orbs, moving shapes and shadows, and other unexplained images. Yes, there are some entities that are not of the spirit realm but when we work they stay in the shadows, angelic celestial light is way too powerful for them, and we are protected and safe in our bubble of light.

This brings me to Slender/Shadow man the nasty energy that had to go. After our Christmas dinner which was delicious by the way, armed with a bag of crystals, seven of us made our way through the maze of corridors until we reached room 7. As soon as we entered you could feel the difference in temperature as it dropped drastically. He knew we were coming. Once I had placed an array of cleansed energised crystals in a circle on the floor, we stepped inside for protection. Crystals hold energy; have many healing properties even though not scientifically proven, lightworkers, healers, and reiki therapists are all aware of the properties of crystals. They can be charged and cleansed by leaving them out in the sun, rinsed through running water, and under a full moon; after all, they come from within our earth. I do not leave my house without wearing them which I have on all the time and believe me; they help to keep negative energies at bay. They are used in electrical gadgets so it shows there is something in it.

Once inside the circle the noises and banging from unseen forces started, it was as if an earthquake was vibrating the floor. Starting with reciting the Lord's Prayer, as the group continued to say it I told the spirit to leave, that he was not wanted here, calling on my guides and protectors to rid The Dolphin of the negative energy. With all spirits, I like to give them a choice to go of their own accord or they will be sent to the light without consent by using Palms 23, The Lord is my shepherd. We continued with the Lord's Prayer asking my guides for help while telling the spirit to leave, the bangs, thumps, and growls became louder, so loud in fact that we had to shout above the noise. Together with Angie Garrard, Mandi Withers, Liz Soppet, Sharon Hunter, Tracy Markwick, Sarah Mann and I, we filled the room with our voices, good was overcoming evil. Do not show fear with negative energies as they feed on fear and do not provoke, would you poke a grizzly bear standing in front of you?... It was a battle of wills for over an hour, a portal of light had opened up on the ceiling and the spirit was informed that if we say palms 23 three times he will be sucked up without a choice. The room temperature was at freezing point by now, our hands clasped tightly to form a circle of strength and together we recited The Lord is my Shepherd, all the while telling him to go back to Binstead wood, once gone he can never return to The Dolphin or he would go up to the light. Knowing that this spirit had committed crimes against humanity on the earth plane we knew for him this was not a good option. By the time we had finished reciting it the 2nd time there was a crescendo of loud bangs and then silence. Stillness fell across the room and the temperature began to rise. The Slender man had gone. Love and light prevails.

The groups are progressing so much that hopefully later in 2020 they will be taking part in a fledgling evening, COVID permitting! This is held in spiritual churches to give them experience in working from a podium giving messages to people in the congregation. Once they are confident within themselves they can then serve the churches on their own, if the churches feel their abilities are good enough to give comfort to the people who attend.

We also work on the philosophy side of spirituality, the podium is not just about delivering messages, it is also about inspirational readings, writings and addresses sending love and light to everyone and acknowledging karma and retribution. What goes around truly comes around, worth remembering, if you want to bad mouth someone or wish them bad luck or worse because it will bite you on the backside two-fold. Dodgy ex's, someone causing pain and harm, stealing, in fact, any negative actions, send out love and light and let karma do the rest. Believe me, it does exist, the old proverb: you reap what you sow also expressed as: as you sow, so shall you reap. If I have learned anything from the dead, karma is real. It may not happen straight away but it will happen and here's the thing you cannot run from it either, in this life or the next.

As you work within the circle and if the connection is right for you, eventually you all work together and will be able to pick up what the others are feeling from the spirit that comes through and hear the messages given. Like any muscle, and the brain is definitely one, the more you work and open up there is the likelihood of a headache or two but they will eventually subside as you spiritually progress.

No pain no gain, I feel truly grateful with what I do and the comfort that I give to people is amazing and so rewarding.

It does make me laugh when some people think it is the work of the devil but are still eager for a message! Also when people preach if it is a gift from God you should give it freely, well the same could be said about singers, songwriters, inspirational writers, leaders, artists, etc. I don't see multimillion-pound recording artists rushing to give their music away for free, or the bloke who wrote 'How to become a millionaire' giving his book away, that would be defeating the obvious.... Just saying! With any ability, it is about working and developing it, and in my case, it is my job and everybody needs to pay their bills and put food on the table.

Here is a thought, when you look at films like, Avatar, Sixth Sense, Ghost, in fact, anything psychic, ghostly and spiritual, books, programmes and artist interpretation, they all started from a dream, inspiration, a thought process which is how spirit communicate.... makes you wonder....are spirit trying to tell us something?... We just need to listen, people can be so blinkered it stops them opening up to other possibilities. I am so glad that I work with spirit by opening up the rewards are truly amazing and I do not mean monetary, knowing that every lesson in life has to be dealt with to learn and grow, there are no short cuts. I personally believe through my guides that we decide what challenges we face in life before we are even born, no one else. Our soul's development leads to our general well being, however hard the obstacles we have to overcome. Our freedom of choice and earthly emotions including self-doubt, fear, anxiety, procrastinating, stubbornness, jealousy, lust, pride, laziness, anger, being judgemental and extreme greed for wealth or material things, can stop us reaching our true potential and deters us off the pathway originally intended. I never feel alone; know that death is not the end, that in fact, every end has a new beginning.

CHAPTER 8

Liquid refreshment with a spirit or ten

T he bar area of The Dolphin is very bohemian, there are two entrances, giving it two addresses and two very different atmospheres. The one in Surrey Street used to be the main entrance for the hotel. The open front door area and stairs leading up into the hotel where the private accommodation was part of the guest rooms, has long since gone. Now there is a partitioning wood and glass wall with a door either side. This end of the bar is light bright and welcoming. The other entry in the High Street takes you to a smaller section of the bar with a raised seating area which is the cellar end, it feels more oppressive. On the raised area there are military uniforms, one of which is RAF uniform; this is inhabited by a friendly airman who tends to salute when he knows you can see him. The other army uniform has also got a lodger but he seems to be a bit grumpy or perhaps they had a tiff when I went in!

Also on the raised area at the table near the step, an old fashioned Victorian man complete with a top hat can sometimes be seen counting money, change rattling and the chinking of coins can often be heard. Stacks upon stacks of coins appear as he writes in a ledger. Perhaps calculating the day's takings and when he is finished he literally sinks down into the cellar beneath, probably counting stock. Through transfiguration and the Ouija board, he has said his name is Thomas;

Thomas Staples was a formidable gentleman who was the landlord at The Dolphin Hotel. He is on the census form 1851 as the Victualler. Thomas and his wife Charlotte had 7 children, 3 of which died in infancy; Lavina who has not come forward, however both Maryann and Clara's presence has been felt and they have communicated via the Ouija. Even though they died before Thomas came to The Dolphin they undoubtedly followed their beloved parents. Thomas Jr, known as Tom worked with his father looking after the wine barrels, has also come through on the Ouija, Fred Batt from The Haunted Experience communicated with him last year. Thomas Staples's descendant Jenny Wright has come forward with information on how he acquired The Dolphin and a painting of him posing as an Ostler before he came to the hotel which is on The Haunted Dolphin Hotel Facebook pages. I instantly recognised him as the spirit who pops in from time to time to count his money and stock, Ellie has also felt his presence. It is believed that Thomas was a steward on the Norfolk Estate and was given The Dolphin for services rendered. Was it because of his dealings with the smugglers and turning a blind eye? Was The Dolphin the epicentre of the dodgy dealings? Only Thomas knows that! Is that why he pops in now and then to count his profits and overlook his contraband stacking up in the cellar? A thrifty businessman in life and now a shrewd protector in death!

There was something amazing at this end of the bar too. On a singles night in May 2019, one of the guests was talking to a medium in the bar, namely me. We were talking about life after death and I was explaining we decide when our expiry date will be before we come on to the earth plane, unless we behave irrationally or dangerously, take our own life, or like the corona virus which can cause massive losses to mankind. We also decide what lessons we learn in this lifetime. Unfortunately, it is not until death that some spirits realise they picked way too soon to die. The gentleman's wife had died a year ago to the day, hence, why he was asking the questions. Just after I was talking to him he walked to the toilet at the end of the bar and what appeared to be a small Angel flew out of the table, it was by his left side as it went up to the ceiling and disappeared. This was caught on CCTV which you will find on The Haunted Dolphin Hotel and also The L.I.G.H.T Paranormal Team Facebook page. Ellie being the paranormal investigator that she is has tried to re-enact the event with no signs of our angelic friend. There was no chance of any reflections, the hat the gentleman was wearing is a cowboy hat with no reflective sides and the video has been checked to see if it has been tampered with. If you can, have a look and see what you think. Coincidence or not the timing could not have been planned better and on a journey to the toilets that this regular has done many times before without any sign of what was showing on the video. I like to see it as a message from his late wife to say it's ok to move on, that she is still right by his side watching over him.

In between the door to the men's toilets and the bar hatch, there is a cupboard pushed up tight against the wall where you will find all kinds of memorabilia. Just recently the CCTV caught the items being pushed off the side by invisible hands. The barmaid who was working behind the bar and heard the noise as they fell to the ground can clearly be seen looking bemused and searching the bar for any possible culprit. The video can be found on The Haunted Dolphin Hotel and also The L.I.G.H.T Paranormal Team Facebook page.

When you walk into the right-hand door from Surrey Street you will find a pool table where a spirit black and white dog can often be seen roaming around, Lord Byron's dog Boatswain perhaps popping in with his master for a quickie? It has been the cause of a little bit of heated conversation when people were not allowed to bring their dogs in. For this was one dog that did not beg for scraps and any whoopsie mishaps didn't leave a trace! Now dogs are greeted with a full doggy menu making them feel right at home. There is more about Lord Byron in chapter 12.

Smugglers were rife at this time especially as the river used to run near to The Dolphin even though it was rerouted in 1735 when it was rebuilt. After several attempts, judging by the catacomb of tunnels behind the outside wall of The Dolphin, the smugglers eventually created a tunnel that came up into the cellar and the bar above just inside the main door. There was an underground smugglers tunnel with a large hole that used to be in the middle of the bar. The boat used to flow underneath and the smugglers would climb up with their booty of contraband, brandy, and tobacco. The tunnels would link all the pubs together from The Crown, The Gratwick, The Globe in the middle, The Dolphin, The White Hart and down to The Britannia on the key side by the river Arun where they used to moor their boats, the ever receptive landlords would always be waiting. The cellar still floods twice a day because of the old river bed, always at the same place except when perhaps a divine intervention brought the Ouija boards to light by causing mass flooding. It was while smugglers were in the tunnels that it collapsed. Sailor songs can be heard along with barrels rolling and the sound of rushing water when the tide is out. When the pedestrian precinct replaced the road outside The Dolphin on the high street, small bones were found in a manmade tunnel which was believed to be that of a 15-year-old smuggler who still haunts The Dolphin today called Billy. Surprisingly, there was a woman who used to run the smuggling racket which was confirmed by an historian interested in Littlehampton. In addition to the tunnel, she would go around the bars wearing a huge skirt where a large proportion of the contraband was hidden.

There is a bike in the bar mounted on the wall by the ladies toilet dating back to around 1940s; it was found abandoned in a shed which Ellie brought from a tinker. An old man is often seen riding his bike without a care in the world on a journey to somewhere, a ghost travelling on a time loop playing over and over again?

The toilets are also an interesting place to be, surprisingly, they smell like cherry pie and home-cooked food when Jane the old cook resides there. This is where the kitchen used to be so when you open the door she can often be heard yelling, "Get out of my kitchen!" On a sour note, ladies frequenting the toilet have found themselves looking at a woman's reflection in the mirror. In some unlucky cases, they have been pushed right up against the mirror, they then have needed help because they cannot physically pull themselves away to get up straight again. Obviously, their need to use the loo was greater than listening to Jane, bet they will think again next time...

A friend of Ellie's who is a sceptic rang her and asked if she could look at the CCTV. Whilst he was standing at the bar he had seen something moving out of the corner of his eye, he wanted to see if anything was picked up knowing the history of The Dolphin. Ellie looked at the recording and saw an arm forming, a leg, then the body and face in fact the whole figure was before her on the screen, and it looked like a little imp. Now imps are the lowest form in the demonic spectrum of things, nothing scary about that at all! Ellie was shocked, so just to check she wasn't going mad it was sent off to a Paranormal Investigation Unit who checks out on all things unexplained. The video was validated as being authentic and the little imp has been Googled, watched, and shared all over the world, even being the No 1 spot in a combination of videos for the spookiest places! If you haven't got Facebook to view it on The Haunted Dolphin Hotel or The L.I.G.H.T Paranormal page, then check out the episode of Help! My House Is Haunted.

A regular of the bar who would often mock the rumours of the hotel being haunted sat one night happily drinking his beer; he again was mocking the supposed spirit clientele with his new drinking buddy, well until he simply disappeared before his very eyes! Needless to say, he was no longer a sceptic.

Swirling shapes, directional orbs, and moving shadows are often caught on the CCTV, well the karaoke is fabulous and who wouldn't want to dance to the tunes blaring out.

The bar is full of memorabilia that Ellie has collected over the years, including an accordion that was stolen from the bar by a young man last year 2019, but the accordion can still be heard. Perhaps he will get his karma. Many of the objects have attachments or residue energy from the past, these attachments can cause sensations, unexplained drafts, energies, mood swings, noises, in fact, anything unnatural. The sound of a music box was heard behind the bar by the Most Haunted Experience which is mentioned in chapter 14. There is no music box in The Dolphin but the residual is still there just like the accordion, the gramophone, and the piano which can also play in the stillness of the night from time to time. I am sure the mischievous spirits play 'Roll out the barrel', the amount of time the barrels roll on the ceiling in room 7!

The lady in white is often seen behind the bar, a regal figure she makes, and in fact, you often get a glimpse of her in various places in The Dolphin. Mark Green from The L.I.G.H.T Paranormal Team and also a regular at The Dolphin has seen a full-bodied apparition of the lady in white floating from one closed internal door out into the bar area. On a recent lone Jack the Ripper themed ghost hunt while on lockdown she was captured on a live feed, her white mist floating past which had Ellie screaming and running in the opposite direction.

Behind the bar seems to be a hive of activity, things tend to move, glasses fall off the side and little, wet, child-sized footprints are often found. Then there is Dickie the cabin boy who likes to serenade the punters, bar staff, and entertain the ghost hunters by copying the tunes they whistle. His tunes echo around the bar in various places leaving people mesmerized by the unexplained sound. Who needs music and karaoke when you have Dickie, cool right!

The welcoming log fire is a sight to behold especially on cold winter nights that is if you can get close enough. A ghostly golden Labrador sleeps constantly in front of it. Every time I go in he is still there happy as Larry... not much good as a guard dog though.

Dave, well what can we say about him other than he was picked up by Help! My House Is Haunted. He is a smelly sweaty leery chap, big bald, about 5ft 9 and likes to get close to women. He gives the feeling of a heart attack and tightness in the chest. Often found loitering in the bar except when there are ghost hunting guests, he then likes to follow and cop a feel of the buttocks of ladies while standing up close and personal behind them.

The Jack the Ripper section has a lot of memorabilia too, it is situated in a little cubby-hole in front of the bar, the energy is not necessarily negative but there is certainly a presence. Jack's 2nd victim Annie Chapman stayed at The Dolphin and her spirit pops in from time to time. A place of positive memories of sunshine, sea, and a wee glass of gin rather than the place she met her untimely death. Check out Jack the Ripper séances in chapter 12.

There is also a Titanic section to make Ellie's great, great, great Uncle Reginald Butler feel right at home. He died on the Titanic whilst travelling in 2nd class hoping for a better life. During one of the ghost hunts, a horn-like sound and ringing bells were heard in the cellar, was that spirit mimicking the last sounds of the Titanic before she slipped into the murky depths of the Atlantic Ocean?

Many other spirits are coming and going and treating it just like they would when they were alive. A place to meet locals for friendly chats, a hotel of the well to do, the old nun shouting out 'sinners', serving wenches, dodgy Fagin from the livery days, beggars and drunkards all make up the wonderful energy of The Dolphin. What more could you possibly want? If you ever feel you're being touched up the chances are they are after your wallet!

CHAPTER 9

Down, down into the depth
of the Coffin Room cellar

F ormer chambermaid, Margaret, who used to work in The
Dolphin came to see Ellie in 2007 and asked if she could
have a look around for old time's sake. On the tour Margaret
said to Ellie that her flat had been part of the hotel and that the
stairs had gone; in the bar, under a hatch ceiling, you can find
the top of the stairs. When they went into the front cellar, she
said, "This isn't right, I remember it being just one big cellar. Do
you know what, there used to be a Gentlemen's Club of the elite
that used to have prostitutes, they would eat food and drink
whisky getting up to all kinds of drunken illegal stuff until all
hours of the morning hidden away from the public? We didn't
know what they got up to half the time!" She asked Ellie, "Why
is it all blocked up? It used to be one big cellar with a pit from
when it was a garage and now it has been walled up and filled
in, it doesn't make sense!" Ellie went upstairs and said about
the activities and showed her a book of drawings from a spiritual artist medium. She informed Ellie that there was so much
activity in the hotel that they just tried to ignore it. In those
days work was hard to find so you didn't complain you got on
with the job. Looking through the book she looked at one of the
photographs and screamed, she had recognised one of the pictures of a young girl from her past who had gone missing, "That's
*Maureen! Where did you get the picture from?" Ellie told her
that the artist had picked up on a dead body behind the wall,
and there was also a smell of what appeared to be a gas leak.
Margaret said, "*Maureen went missing from a part of the town
down by the beach and she was a well known prostitute." About
the same time as Margaret had come into the pub four women
in their 60's also came in and the conversations about The Dol-

phin Hotel got Ellie bringing out the book of drawings again. Instantly, when one of the women saw the face of the young lady in the picture she said, "That's *Maureen, what is she doing in there? She went missing from Littlehampton just up the road!"

Ever since Ellie has had the pub there has always been a funny smell in the cellar. Five times she has called the gas man out and each time there was no evidence of a leak. Half joking he told her what you need is a cadaver dog, as a dead body gives off a similar smell to a gas leak! As soon as the gas man said that the smell went, now and then the smell returns. Just by this area is a door leading to stairs that just stop dead seven steps up, they are in line with the hatch up in the ceiling of the bar that is sealed off, where the original stairs leading into the hotel are. This area has a steady stream of orbs coming from it, another portal to the spirit realm? Or are these spirits trapped within the changed structure?

About this time Ellie and The L.I.G.H.T Paranormal Team were conducting more Ouija sessions in the cellar due to the increased activity, during one of the session Ellie asked if there were any spirits buried in here, it responded by spelling out, 'Help, help, trapped, find me!' Mischievous spirits listening in to the conversation and giving false readings? Or is there an actual truth in the matter? Many a medium have been in the cellar and told Ellie not just one but several bodies may be buried within the walls and it feels as if they are being sucked in. On random nights a musket shot can be heard which has been recorded, the smell of singed hair, sulphur, (not a good smell as it symbolises a demonic presence), and the words ashes to ashes can be heard! Just lately there has been a trumpet or horn-like sound. Have lost souls been disposed of by burning to leave no trace?

There is a dark, oppressiveness within the cellar, the feeling of being watched is overwhelming, spine-tingling sensations and goose bumps are pretty much the norm. As you walk in through the door and look to the left, Ellie has boxes of stock and glasses.

The dark shadows behind it feel foreboding, the first time I went in there I said to Ellie, "Does the words 'Devils Gate' mean anything to you?" She looked at me with a shocked expression and said, "Derek Acorrah had said that to her!"

Becoming more and more frequent, the dark burly figure of Thomas stands in the centre when you open the door; he stares at you, and then promptly disappears. Lights flash randomly with no power source, shadow people linger by the walls, whispering can be heard, and again the laughter of children. Whooshes of cold air blast through with no doors open and a feeling of static energy which produces a cobweb sensation.

Walking to the left you go towards the cooling room where the barrels are kept, it is in here I could see the Gentlemen's Club seated at a table, the smell of sweat, cigars, and drink, laughter from both men and women, cards shuffling, coins tinkering, music playing but as it played like a video in my head the energy became more sinister. People took liberties of their position and exploited the vulnerable. This room also fills with orbs... was there more to their meetings? Were unimaginable crimes committed on the helpless? Now and then a nun is seen in an old fashioned habit floating through the cellar; she is heard to repeatedly shout out 'sinners'. Perhaps for the Gentlemen's Club or maybe the events that have happened over the centuries...

There is a door with fencing on blocking off the area to the dumbwaiter, long since condemned due to it falling unexpectedly on Ellie's arm causing it to go black, but not before a brother and sister allegedly fell to their death. Giggling as they hid inside their secret hideaway, the weight of their little bodies was just too much for the dumbwaiter to hold. They were found sometime later after they had fallen, a dull thud can still be heard along with creaks of the wheel that can no longer turn. What started as an innocent game of hide and seek ended in tragedy. The children have come forward often on the Ouija board to tell their tale.

There is a tiny room where the generator is kept which Ellie calls the Safe Cellar, it is anything but! As you go inside stones, tiny teeth and small pieces of glass amongst other things are thrown at you from thin air. William tends to stand over you menacingly. It is behind the wall that backs on to the street that the catacombs of tunnels were found. Were they caused by the smugglers trying and failing on numerous attempts to dig under the foundations to smuggle their booty perhaps? The sensation of cobwebs covers your face with not a web to be seen. An un-explainable event happened on a ghost hunt while in this room which you will find in chapter 14.

Further along the corridor on the right, you will see a hole in the wall where Ellie used an industrial jackhammer to try to see if she could find anything but to no avail, the wall was too thick. Someone did not want us to find out the secrets of the Dolly.... Asking the question to Penji to show me where the dead bodies are, it instantly swings in the direction of the hole. Is it spirit playing with me? Or is it the actual truth of the matter?

At the end of the corridor is where the barrels are thrown down from the delivery Lorries. When you stand near the hatch on ghost hunts, a tingling sensation starts in your legs working its way up into your body with the feeling of being off-balance. Pains in the head, neck, and back are also felt. The reason why this is happening is because of 18-year-old Joseph, he was de-livering the barrels but lost his footing and fell into the hatch and to his death, breaking his neck as the barrels fell upon him, so his spirit and the Ouija board says. Symptoms, however, do not lie!

On a ghost hunt in November 2019, while with 12 guests down by the hatch and feeling the normal sensations associated with Joseph, there was a loud bang. In the main cellar, 6 large gas bot-tles were held in place by 2 giant wooden wedges. The wedges had been scattered across the floor causing the gas bottles to fall and roll across the cellar. Now gas bottles and rolling do not mix. After putting the bottles securely back in place, witnessed by the whole group, we returned to the hatch to conduct further investigations when the same thing happened again. No one else was in the cellar that could have been able to pull out the wedges, they were stuck fast. Will the last person running out the door please turn off the light!

The cameraman John on Help! My house Is Haunted and Barri was down in the cellar when all of a sudden John jumped and screamed. When asked by Barri what was wrong, he said, "There was a woman standing right next to me and she whispered in my ear, what's going on?" This was all caught on camera and can be seen in the program. He seemed petrified, what you didn't see when he went upstairs was him shaking and had to sit down. Surprising really, as previously he had said to Ellie when she questioned why he did this job, he told her he doesn't believe in spirits, 'nothing has happened to me'... guess he has changed his mind then! Barri also felt cobwebs on his face and when he used an SLS camera which maps out an area and picks up spirits showing them as stick people. Two spirits presented themselves on the equipment standing in the doorway of the cellar.

On a ghost hunt with Haunted Houses, which can be found in chapter 15, a spirit used a thick wire that hangs across the ceiling of the cellar to give intelligent answers by moving it to command.

During a mini ghost hunt with Ellie's friends Vicky and her brother, they clearly saw a child's footprint besides a puddle on the cellar floor. The features of the foot were so detailed you could see the shape of each little toe. There is a screenshot from the live feed that was being conducted at that time. There is a photograph and a video on The Haunted Dolphin Hotel and The L.I.G.H.T Paranormal Facebook page.

As mentioned before during diphtheria and influenza epidemics in Littlehampton, the town morgue could not handle the number of corpses that were mounting up. The Dolphin became the place to store the surplus decaying corpses due to the cold damp conditions. Hundreds of bodies were stored along with the spirits attached to them perhaps. No wonder there are countless orbs seen floating around the cellar and hotel, this would have been the last place they called home. During the COVID 19 virus pandemic of 2020, the hotel had been completely been shut down including all equipment due to people being on lockdown. There was no one outside and no other noise pollution, so no explanation for the sound of a baby crying. Ellie, who was conducting a live visual, heard the screams of this poor child in the stillness of the cellar. Restless souls left on the earth plane unsure of where to go once their body had ceased to exist and now forever to remain in the walls of The Dolphin...

My own Angel table is down in the cellar, blessed with holy water it allows the spirit to come through to tell their story. Not only from the spirit that dwells in The Dolphin Hotel but also from loved ones who come through for people on ghost hunts, and also transient spirits that wish to be crossed over. They let us know their stories before they go into the light. One such spirit was a boy called Bradley who died in hospital from cancer aged 6, when his spirit left his body he went around the hospital, by the time he came back his family had gone. He roamed around looking for them until eventually he lived in a house with a man who had a dog and cat but there was another spirit in the house who was not very friendly, so he left. After roaming around for a while, he was drawn to the light of The Dolphin when we were working with spirit and asked if we could return him to his family, happily we crossed him over back to the spirit realm. There have been many children old and new that have been crossed over who have found a voice through the table and been sent to rest.

Sally, Tommy, Thomas, Harry, Dolly is also known as Ada, Robert, Edward, Dickie, Billy, Michael, Rosalind, Katie, David, Jessica, Maryanne, Clara Amelia, Ann, Elizabeth, Annie, Simon,

Albert, Peter, and Sally are just a few of the children who have come through and talk to us now and then. William tries to dominate at times but with the experience of Slender man, he is now dubious because he knows he could be sent up or pushed out. As trying as William can be is still part of The Dolphin and that is the way he wants to keep it.

2nd Cellar

Dark, narrow, stone stairs take you down to the second cellar at the back of The Dolphin. There is a stagnant, pungent smell in this dark, dank, divided room. In the first room, there is a spirit of a teenage girl who was locked away for stealing bread well over a century ago. Huddled in the corner, accidentally or purposely, she starved to death. Only the person responsible knows the answer to that. She calls herself Elizabeth, whether it is fear of the repercussions for her crime she refuses to leave and stays in the room, permanently. There is an old coal shoot long since emptied, except for the loan spirit of a young boy about 8 years old called Thomas. He fell into the shoot and was crushed by the bags of coal that fell on top of him, the dust finishing him off by suffocating the poor soul. You can tell when he is around, the smell of coal is apparent. In the second room, a man proclaims ownership telling anyone who can hear him get off his land. He shows the surrounding area how it used to be long before The Dolphin. It was farming land with wooden huts, ploughed fields, and farm animals. When he is near his energy affects your back from years of toiling on the land perhaps but he is definitely not a happy chappy.

A male energy with a bald head, stocky build very forceful in character, the smell of alcohol and sweat fills the air due to the confined space within the cellar. The smell is overwhelming and nauseating. He tends to stay in the bar area but recently he has found his way down into the 2nd cellar. This gentleman was picked up by the Help! My House Is Haunted team in the bar area called Dave.

An unnatural death also occurred in the cellar, breathing re-striction especially around the neck is often felt when the male energy pops in.

There is also a mirror situated at the bottom of the stairs that seems to be a portal to spirit, when you stand before it you can see rows upon rows of shadow spirit people trying to get out!... This phenomenon has been captured on film which you can find in The Haunted Dolphin Hotel and The L.I.G.H.T Paranormal Facebook pages.

Stones are chucked down the stairs and on leaving this darkly lit cellar there is a sense of being chased, no one can get out quick enough.

* Name has been changed.

CHAPTER 10

Let's play in the garden
after midnight

D riving through the wooden gates into the car park of The
Dolphin, there is a wooden gazebo directly in front of you
near to where Fredrick Holliss, the old landlord, met his end. It
is also where the smokers congregate seeming to be in a rush to
join the spiritual occupants of The Dolphin. Turning to the right
you can park your car in front of an old, flint wall, hundreds of
years old. Spookily the weather-worn stones seem to form the
shape of a dolphin; this was once where part of the livery barn
stood. The barn was where Molly the good-time girl and a stable
boy met their untimely death by way of hanging. Fredrick the
blacksmith made his barrels, amongst other things. Perhaps because his old home was razed to the ground he now resides in
room 7 taking pride in scaring the guests by rolling his barrels.

To the left of where the barn was the garden area is situated,
wooden tables and chairs stand ready for the lazy, hazy days of
summer to enjoy a pint or 10. The old fisherman cottages used
to stand there before joining the barn in being a pile of rubble.
On quiet, still nights, spirit horses have been heard neighing and
stamping their hooves and the sound of children's laughter and
skipping can be heard, with their little ghostly faces shining out
under a full moon as they play hide and seek. Around the back
of the hotel is a doorway that leads to the iron fire escape where
the children have been seen running along and peering into the
rooms. The lady in white also tends to glide past the windows, a
ghostly apparition still searching the grounds for her long, lost
child?

What I find intriguing as a medium, sometimes when I look
down into the garden from the hall stairs window, it is like

going back in time. Hearing the sound of motors and watching old cars going into the garage inspection pit that used to be in the dark, depths of the cellar many years ago, playing on a time loop of a past long since forgotten. Watching bullocks and horses pulling carts laded with goods from many a merchant that would pass this way to the harbour. The sound of cattle mooing, the echo of which Ellie has caught on a recording in room 2, as they were herded down to St. Catherines Field by the slaughterhouse further down the street by their master, who has only just recently made his presence felt in The Dolphin. He has rancid breath and black wooden looking teeth, as if he has a deformity of the mouth, penetrating black eyes, ruddy looking cheeks, negative energy and wide in stature, good looking chap!

Ladies and gentlemen in fine dress, ragamuffin children looking for lost coins, unsavoury sorts standing in the shadows and ladies of the night using the side entrance to visit some punter paying for their wares, but it is the visions of the children that haunt me the most. Over the time in The Dolphin, I have crossed over many spirits that wish to go but there are still so many that stay for it is all they have known, perhaps through fear or just because it is a place they call home.

While doing one of our many ghost hunts, the children have spoken, giving their tales of how they have passed through disease, poverty, fire, accident, abuse, past battles from many, many centuries ago and drowning, just some of the things these poor souls have suffered. The garden has an eeriness all of its own. On more than one occasion while using the Ouija a couple of children have described their final resting place as the garden.... is that why so many play in the shadows? A past when children had no place, they were exploited back through the centuries. Or is it just mischievous spirits adding to the ambience of The Dolphin, keeping the suspense and secrets of a long since forgotten past? After all, the land has been here since time forgot, it appears that The Dolphin holds near the ones who have fallen on the land, drawing others spirits in with the energy it omits, good and bad.

CHAPTER 11

Little Dolly

The presence of little Dolly was becoming apparent with the playful mischievous antics that were happening around The Dolphin. Things would go missing then reappear in the same place a few days later, followed by laughter at Ellie's expense due to the frustration she felt when these items went missing. Doors would open then suddenly shut, light sounding footsteps running up and down the corridors, even behind the bar. Ellie and her staff member Mel found one small child's footprint on the floor as if the child had just got out of the bath, with no explanation why. As mentioned before, Ellie named her little Dolly because everyone used to call The Dolphin Hotel the Dolly, so it felt natural to call her that. Dolly loves girls with red hair, staff members have had their hair pulled and been tickled, but never maliciously. Ellie is strongly protective over little Dolly and regards her as the daughter she never had, a wonderful, vulnerable little girl. Dolly does not like William, in fact, all the children are dubious of him and tend to disappear when he is around, perhaps because of what he has done in the past or the fact his energy can be just plain nasty.

Ada Constance Parrish was a young girl who lived at The Dolphin Hotel with her father the landlord, her mother, and siblings. There was an outbreak of diphtheria around the turn of the 20th century and when the children got sick; to keep them cool they would take them down to the cellar. Ada Parish hated it in the cellar, she was afraid of it because of the atmosphere and how damp and cold it was. Ada begged her parents to take her back upstairs into the hotel, against their better judgment they took her back up to the nursery. Unfortunately, perhaps a result of that she died in 1906 aged 6 in the nursery, room 7. There is a gravestone in the local cemetery which Ellie was not aware of until a gentleman searching his family tree came across some very interesting information. His Grandfather was a landlord at The Dolphin in the early 1900's and had 14 children, one of them had died in the nursery, Ada, she was buried in the local cemetery. Ellie went along to see where she was buried, upon finding the grave she found Ada Constance Parish written on the tombstone and in adverted comers was the nickname 'Dolly' named after The Dolphin Hotel.

When Derek Acorah visited in 2006 filming for Ghost Towns he felt Dolly's presence too, holding out his hand he said he felt her energy as her ghostly fingers entwined with his, describing her as having pigtails and died with something to do with the throat. It was six months after Derek's visit that the gentleman who led Ellie to Dolly's grave had come into the bar with a carrier bag full of photos of the children. Inside one of which was Dolly, when he showed Ellie the photograph the little girl had pigtails. Dolly's picture can be found at the end of the book.

It was after this revelation that Ellie recruited a medium she knew and took her to room 7 to investigate the nursery. Both the medium and ghost hunting equipment was telling her to look in the built-in cupboard which led her to a crawl space behind one of the walls. Ellie climbed into the back where she found some shards of glass in a sack when she put them all together they formed the negative photo of little Dolly, the one the relative had shown her. Ellie said on finding it, "People slate the paranormal but then all the evidence comes together like a jigsaw puzzle."

Dolly loves to interact with people especially on ghost hunts. Communicating on the Ouija board is one of her favourite things, especially when using a drawing planchette with a pen attached. Using the energy of the guest she draws hearts showing she is just a friendly, playful spirit wanting attention and love. The coldness felt in room 7 from Dolly and the other children is when they come very close yearning to be loved and hugged.

To realise that Dolly was actually a living breathing person is spine-tingling enough but now in death, she continues to be part of The Dolphin, Ellie is very protective of her. She can appear as a black-eyed child but that may be more to do with what she looked like when she died, rather than a demonic entity. Showing that spirit can be misunderstood, being a demonic energy could not be further from the truth, she is just an innocent child who feels she is home.

CHAPTER 12

The famous and infamous spirit cast of The Dolphin Hotel

Here is a recap on some of the spirits found in The Dolphin; the list is endless as there is a constant stream of newbies and visitors. These are the ones that have been seen the most and interact with the living.

Little Dolly, The Dolphin's sweetheart, we all love Dolly. She appears in various places all over the hotel. Gentle, playful, protective, she pulls hair, especially when it's long and colourful and she loves to talk through the Ouija table. Dolly also likes to draw hearts by using a planchette with a pencil attached. She giggles, skips, sings and likes to sit on people's laps or by their legs in the psychic circle.

William haunts everywhere he feels he is the proprietor of the hotel. He is very oppressive, doesn't like strong women, especially Ellie as she is the landlady and undermines his stature, or so he thinks. He causes lights to go out randomly especially in the toilets, chucks things around, smashes glasses, lies to mediums and anyone who will listen or talk to him on the Ouija boards, and makes himself out to be the victim. He stands so close you can feel his negativity overwhelming anyone he goes near. People who have worked in the hotel have felt scared and left. William allegedly was hanged for raping his niece Jane and strangling her. When he comes too close the feeling of being strangled can be felt, it feels as if a rope or hand is around your neck, people on ghost hunts and in the psychic circle experience the same sensation. His picture can be found in the photograph section drawn by a spiritual artist.

Jane was The Dolphin Hotel cook; she died at 32 years of age when she was brutally raped and murdered. Jane shares her story often on ghost hunts telling anyone who will talk with her that her Uncle William killed her. However, he is always quick to disagree and swears his innocence... I know who I believe! Jane's scream can still be heard from time to time along with a whimpering sound. She tends to haunt the ladies toilet which was where the kitchen used to be, only coming out when people are on the Ouija board so she can be heard or when other negative entities are at play. Customers have had things thrown at them including toilet rolls, and her black boot has been seen, and then disappears.

The governess/nanny roams the corridor and inside room 7, perhaps checking on her wards and all the spirit children that remain in The Dolphin Hotel. When we are conducting ghost hunts she often comes in to offer her protection from the many negative energies that show up every now and then, especially to protect the children, dedicated to her job even in death.

Fredrick Holliss, the popular land lord who jumped to his death likes his presence to be known on ghost hunts. Many people have commented that they feel as if something is trying to draw them to the window. Did the numerous spirits of The Dolphin lure him to his death? Will we ever know the actual truth of the matter? At times when he has come through he is incoherent. Is the same mental health issue affecting him in life still plaguing him in death? Hopefully we will find out... one day!

Another Fredrick was the black smith who worked in the stables at the back of The Dolphin. He stays in room 7 protecting the children perhaps, or is there another more sinister reason? He growls, groans, moans and his energy is very intimidating. Bangs, clanging and rolling barrels can be heard when he is around.

Cattle man is a very dark energy; he would take the cattle to be slaughtered by St. Catherines Field. He has rancid breath and smells of sweat so you know when he is around. Portly in size, has a very unnerving stare with black penetrating eyes, ruddy looking cheeks, and what appears to be a deformity around the mouth from ill fitted or broken wooden teeth, after being kicked in the mouth in revenge perhaps from one of his charges going to be slaughtered. Hanging cattle carcases comes into your mind when he appears. When Ellie was doing a live ghost hunt in room 7 during the lockdown, she started doing a transfiguration and as her face started changing, immediately she could feel cattle man by her side. Not a pleasant experience as she promptly stopped. The live can be seen on The Haunted Dolphin Hotel and The L.I.G.H.T Paranormal Facebook page.

Molly worked as a barmaid come chambermaid and is often found in the bar going from table to table chatting up the locals. Molly can also be found in the hotel rooms as she goes around doing her chamber maid duties. She desperately wanted to be loved so would give her wears so easily to anyone who would have her. When she thought she had found the love of her life, it appears it was not reciprocated; for once again she was rejected by the lover who jilted her. Distraught she entered the old stable block and took her own life by hanging. When Molly is about the sensation of restrictions around the neck can be felt and weeping for her lost love can be heard. She has been seen where the stables once where, as mentioned previously, looking like she was wading though water due to the buildings reconstruction.

Tom the stable boy was a teenage of about 17 years old and another victim of hanging, his spirit pops in from time to time in different areas of The Dolphin. Why he died is still uncertain, did someone end his life? Was he in the wrong place at the wrong time? Or was his life so unbearable he committed suicide? The truth is still waiting to be revealed.

Alice, known as the 'Lucky Bag' woman appears in a black dress and bonnet carrying a basket full of assorted flowers, apples and other surprises for the children who seem to follow her wherever she goes. She suffered from sciatica, back pain and arthritis.

Outside The Dolphin there used to be a tree that was a pick up and drop off for the local postman, Alice would sit under the tree handing out gifts to the children of the town. In death she still continues to look after them within the walls of The Dolphin.

Thomas Robert Holliss, known as Robert, a burly landlord in 1907 still pops in from time to time, large in stature and round smiling face with a happy disposition. He was a happy chappy who was always laughing in life and is just the same in death. Two landlords of the same family at different times used to run The Dolphin; he was the uncle of Fredrick Holliss. However, completely different characters and deaths, life took Robert but Fredrick decided his own fate by jumping out the window.

Elizabeth Jane the buxom cook and wife of Thomas Robert Holliss, loiters on the second floor near the toilets by room 3. Wearing her white, mop cap and long kitchen dress, a curvaceous waist from all the delicious food she cooked. A big, smiley, round face and warm energy she is always a joy to bump in to. The sound of dishes and cutlery is often heard in the rooms and corridors, a ghostly memory of the food she dished up being delivered via room service.

The lady in white is often seen roaming around The Dolphin as if she is looking for something. She came through on a session with the Ouija board where Ellie asked her if she was the women in white who walks through walls, the woman told Ellie 'yes' she was also looking for her baby. Directly after that a crying baby could be heard more prominently behind the cavity wall just before room 7, on the left hand side. Mark investigated and found that there is actually a walk way in the cavity. On another session with the lady in white it came out that she had a baby in secret, in those days you could hide your figure easily in the bustle dresses. Whilst hiding the baby girl, the child died. Racked with remorse from her death and for not being able to give her a proper burial the lady continues her quest. Once Ellie had acknowledged the baby and showed empathy for her loss, the baby stopped crying, but still the lady continues to search in vain for her daughter, consumed by grief.

Jack the Ripper's victims; every year a séance is conducted at Halloween to contact one of the victims of Jack the Ripper. Why I hear you ask? Well come closer and I will tell...Jack the Ripper's 2nd victim, Annie Chapman allegedly stayed at The Dolphin Hotel....ahhh I hear you say. Anyway, she had consumption otherwise known as T.B. For half a crown they would pile the poor people onto a cart to bring them down to the coast when the sanatoriums were full, thinking that the sea air would cure them. Annie had stayed in 1886; she was estranged from her husband and had lost a child. Drowning her sorrows in gin she became a hopeless alcoholic. Her death warrant was already signed as very few recovered from consumption, if she hadn't felt the knife of Jack the Ripper, her illness would have sadly claimed her life instead. She died in September 1888, found in the backyard of 29 Hanbury Street. Interestingly enough, at the séance in 2018 when Ellie said, "The gin is open, come on ladies tell us your story." Ellie brought the thoughts feeling and emotions through of the 4th victim Catherine Eddowes and began sobbing uncontrollably. This was even before the actual hypnosis of the willing participant, Ellie conducted this having been learning hypnoses for a year prior to the séance. The willing guest who went under is now working as a medium due to the experience she had. The night also consisted of the séance and ended with a ghost hunt. The whole hotel bar is closed to customers and decorated to enhance the ambience of Victorian London. I had the absolute pleasure of joining in on the 2019 séance and what an experience it was. Being a qualified hypnotherapist, I was able to conduct a series of susceptibility tests, firstly the lemon; taking people on a journey to their fridge and eating a lemon. Magnetic hands; speaks for itself where your hands are drawn together by an apparent magnetic force. Bucket and balloon; there is an imaginary bucket filling with water on one hand and on the other is a balloon filled with helium, and lastly the pendulum; the person who could make it swing using just their energy with their hands completely still. These tests were conducted to find the guest who was most open to hypnoses. One lady was perfect, using hypnoses I took her back to the days of Jack the Ripper and the streets of London. She described what she saw, how she felt, what she was dressed in, the sounds and smells of the pubs and a ship on the Thames. It was a wonderful touch to the evening and enjoyed by all. Ironically as I took her back in time all the other guests susceptible to hypnoses experienced similar things. Was this all Jack the Rippers victims trying to communicate their experiences through the guests due to them being so varied?

The next thing was the séance, as we sat around in a circle asking anyone from the past to come through, Annie Chapman spoke up through me. Being a trance medium she spoke and acted in a way that could not have been further away from my personality to say the least. She made a few people blush, including me when I was told what she said afterwards! Look out for the next one, and then you can find out first hand. The whole night was amazing and well worth coming along to be part of the experience.

Another bad boy Lord Byron the English poet who was known as bad, mad and dangerous to the ones that knew him, frequented The Dolphin Hotel in the summer of 1806 between August the 20th and 30th. Arriving by trusty steed he tethered his horse in the barn at the back of The Dolphin. Letters sent by Byron to his lover Caroline Lamb at that time confirmed that he did indeed have a jolly good time at The Dolphin and preferred that to The Beach Hotel. (The only other hotel at that time in Littlehampton) Lord Byron said when asked, "Why wouldn't you stay at the more opulent Beach Hotel?" He answered, "When visiting a dirty little town I like to stay in dirty little hotels," and The Dolphin Hotel at that time was exactly that. Charming! No doubt he had his hanky on his head, trousers rolled up with his bucket and spade in hand, well just before he nearly drowned in the mouth of the river Arun! He was having a break from the arduous studies as an undergraduate at Cambridge University with his mate Edward Long, playing cricket, shooting pistols and swimming. One visit proved to be a close escape indeed. The harbour in Littlehampton is renowned for its strong interchangeable currents, while swimming too close to the entrance of the harbour it nearly sucked him in. He was then accompanied soaking wet with his trusty dog Boatswain in tow. Every now and then his spirit pops in to room 4 along with Edward for a bit of R&R, to relive again happier times perhaps with Boatswain nipping into the bar too. Proof of his visit includes letters and documents that state he was staying at The Dolphin Hotel. Byron's best work was done in his 20's; perhaps the old Dolly was his inspiration.

Dickie the cabin boy is another spirit who has made himself increasingly more known; he fell overboard during a storm and drowned in the 1700's. When he came through on the Ouija board we could smell and taste sea water, he said he was a good boy and I truly believe he was. His actual name was Richard, tall for his age of 10 and slim in build, he can be heard whistling in various places, especially behind the bar at the entrance to the cellar where you can feel as if he is blowing into your face... He will happily copy the tunes you whistle to him. Even when no one is in there day or night he has been heard when staff have opened up, in mid flow of a melody. His lost soul riding the waves to The Dolphin drawn by the spiritual energy of the portal perhaps, to a place he now calls home. There has been so much evidence captured on recordings from many well known ghost hunting groups. Update: Just before the lockdown from the corona virus, on a session with the Ouija board with one of my psychic circles, witnessed by Yvie Lomer, Christine Canneaux, Scarlet Gard, Janet Budgen-Ashton, Theresa Hawkins and Vici Byrne. Dickie asked to be crossed over. He was standing before us pouting like a petulant child with his arms crossed as I was reluctant to do it because of his amazing activity and positive energy. However, it is not my place to refuse a request I am there to help spirit, he was now ready to pass over and as a group we happily obliged to send him into the light. He did promise that one of the other children would take his place; we will have to see if that is the case.

Prudence first showed herself on a ghost hunt in room 3, wearing a long skirt, pleated blouse with a smart cropped jacket of the early 1800's era. I had my portable Angel board which spirit can talk through and with spiritual manipulation of the K2's, she was able to tell her story. Being a lady of the night for want of a better phrase, she was booked for her wares by one of her regulars. On noticing she was with child, in a jealous rage and using his full weight, he pushed Prudence down onto the bed crushing her as he strangled her until the last breath left her body. It was not until a few weeks later that she spelled out her name on the Ouija boards and confirmed again all the information while on a psychic circle exercise.

Thomas Staples one of the many landlords from the 1800's, counts his pennies in the front bar dressed in Victorian suit complete with a top hat. Dark penetrating eyes and foreboding presence, he likes to sink down into the cellar where he is probably counting his stock. He enjoys intimidating anyone who can see him as he stands and stares when you go into the cellar, protecting his booty no doubt.

Tom as he was known, is Thomas Staples Jr. He seemed to have more of a presence in the early days and has been documented. He was described as a gentleman who used to look after the barrels of wine. After not seeming to contribute on any hauntings we wondered if he had decided to hang up his ghostly cap and retire back to spirit. Perhaps the overbearing character of William had forced him to hide in the shadows or take up residence elsewhere! However, Fred Batt of Most Haunted fame brought this spirit through on the Ouija board in October 2019 while holding a Most Haunted Experience at The Dolphin Hotel.

Harry the dashing airman is normally seen in his RAF uniform, who doesn't love someone dressed up in a uniform! Tall, slim, dark coloured hair with a handle bar moustache he really is quite debonair, roaming around The Dolphin popping up with his protective air. He likes to have a chat on the Ouija board and shows his presence through transfiguration.

Jeremiah is a huge mountain of a man about 6ft 8in tall and normally stands in the corridors that leads to room 7 and the landings. He wears a sea faring outfit more like a smuggler, dark features with dark hair and looks in his late 20's. He seems like a mild manner simpleton, who is always surrounded by spirit children. They feel protected by him, not a threat at all but he can be a bit unnerving due to his size.

Zac is a little boy about 8 years old who nipped in to see Ellie in her living accommodation. Ellie woke up suddenly and saw him suspended above her looking down. He is seen in the pub often playing with the other children. A medium artist drew his face which can be found on the Facebook page. On seeing this picture I recognised him as being the little boy who stuck his tongue out at me while twisting his ears the first time I went into The Dolphin.

Imps: When they pop up in a place they are marking, negative energies that pray on our weaknesses and magnify them. They are about 2-3 feet tall and if ones about, there will be others looming in the crawl spaces and attics. They are sent in by the bigger, dodgier demons to mess with the people within their home. Imps can appear as children, the more experienced mediums can tell the difference between the energies.

Edward who came through on the Ouija board died after his house was bombed in the Second World War. He was looking for his bike that had been outside when the bomb struck. He had been living at The Dolphin ever since. After coming through he decided to come home with me, he knew I would look after him. Not long after his arrival during one of my circles he was picked up by Tony Petretta and asked if he could be crossed over as he was ready to go. Together with Tony, Tracey Skeet, Hazel Booty and Yvie Lomer and I, we crossed Edward back over into the light riding his bike as he went...

A male energy called Thomas also made his presence known as he manipulated the K2's in a question and answer session which was later confirmed on the Ouija table. In the 1700's Thomas was on the run for committing murder, his friend Anthony who worked at the hotel hid him in one of the attic spaces but because of the threat of punishment for harbouring a criminal, he disposed of Thomas himself. Anthony also came through on the Ouija board seeming to be stuck in The Dolphin where he committed his crime.

Annie a young teenage of 14 years old was walking back from an errand for her mum and ended up being abducted off the streets well over a hundred years ago. She gave the initials A.B.G, was this her initials or was it for the name of the guest that liked young children? When she shows herself she has long dark hair with the front strands pulled back into a ponytail. A white flowing long dress, white socks and what looks like black patent boots or shoes. She still carries her little bag in her hand. After the guest was done with her he strangled her. When Annie came through on the table the lights started flashing.

A mischievous spirit called John normally loiters in room 2, he is skinny looking with folic challenged hair resulting in the monks look, dressed in what appears to be a loose top and trousers with an early 1800's look, and breath of a sewage pit. He died of head trauma; he was punched to the ground, while laying on the floor the murderer straddled his chest and hit him with a blunt object. When you are in room 2 you can feel the tight chest from being restricted and shooting pains in the head.

Queenie was 27 years of age, a lady of the night who frequented The Dolphin often for a paying john or two, except one night she stayed here permanently. There was more than one client who was willing to sample her wares with things getting out of hand. She was drowned in the bath; her body was burned and buried within the grounds of the hotel. Queenie is one of many prostitutes that tend to come forward to tell us how easily disposable they were over the years. Being a busy port for many a sailor, it is hardly surprising that the little town on the south coast has many a skeletons within it very dark history.

Peter and Sally are the children who fell to their death in the dumbwaiter while playing hide and seek. Sally likes to join in with the psychic circles and sits on the attendees laps but rather than that warm snugly feeling you get from the living, it is more like sitting in a freezer as you lose the feelings in your legs from the cold. Peter loves to come through on the Ouija just to say hello.

Charlie a teenage boy from the 1300's lived on the land long before The Dolphin was built. The land was used for farming with small settlements scattered with minimalistic wooden houses. He died with all his family and his beloved dog buried in one of the many plague pits. At that time they did not believe in life after death so did not go to the light, their spirits became stuck on the earth plane just to wander in no man's land. They knew we had crossed over other spirits while in the hotel so when Charlie came through with his family they wanted to be crossed over too. With the help of one of my circles we crossed them back into the spirit realm with his dog following behind them. As mediums, we can see them crossing over, the warmth and happiness they feel once they cross is overwhelming with a wonderful sense of peace.

Lily died in the 1700's before the hotel was built. She was in her 20's and buried within 5 miles of The Dolphin, alive, as they thought she was a witch. She now lives within the walls, long red hair, bare feet flowing dress and Irish gypsy heritage. Music can be heard when she is around.

The first time I saw Tommy was on the blocked off stairs in the barrel room in the cellar, he was rolling his ball down the stairs.

He is a playful little boy, small in stature about 6-7 years old who craves attention. You can guarantee when a ghost hunt or live feed is on he will be nearby playing with his ball.

Uma was about 8 years old and from the late 1500's, wearing tatty old clothes and bare feet; he was a powder monkey boy who manned the cannons on warships. The main part of his job was to carry the gunpowder from the powder magazine in the ships hold to where the cannons were situated. When he came through I could see the Spanish flag of the armada and the sound of a pan pipe. This explains why sometimes you can hear whispering in a foreign language. During an intense battle he was hit in the gut from the exploding wood and fell into the sea, his body drifting until he reached the shore. He was originally sold by his parents because they were poor but he loved his life because he was as free as a bird and loved the sea. He has been on the land ever since.

Albert or Bertie as he likes to be known is the alleged owner of the small bones found in the chimney. Seen by Ellie, wearing rags crouched down under the table in the function room, smelling of soot. Children used to be exploited; boys and sometimes girls were used by chimney sweeps as 'climbing boys'. They would shimmy up the narrow flues in the chimney and brush the soot down, if they were not quick enough the chimney sweep would light the fire to speed them up. Unfortunately, Bertie became stuck, suffocated and was then left behind by an uncaring master where children were classed as disposable assets.

Another young boy called Thomas aged 8 who delivered the goal got stuck in the coal shoot as bags of coal fell on top of him, the poor boy suffocated and crushed to death. He stands up close and personal when guests visit the Coffin Room cellar. Is he the one who chucks small stones for attention?

Sophia was a young girl who came through during one of the ghost hunts, she died in a fire with 3 of her siblings, whether it was in The Dolphin is unclear. The date she gave was 1827 which was before the fire in 1828. While trying to sleep smoke engulfed her, she remembered shouting out, 'Mummy, mummy,' then she suffocated and now lives within the walls of The Dolphin, perhaps finding sanctuary with the other spirits

Billy the 15 years old smuggler boy whose bones were found in a tunnel when the town centre precinct was being built. His spirit finding its way to The Dolphin to join the other smugglers in song who also met there untimely end in the smugglers tunnels.

Another Elizabeth lives in the Coffin Room where the coal shoot is. She was 13 years old and had stolen some bread, not long after The Dolphin was built. She was placed in the cellar as punishment for her crime and was left there, perhaps forgotten, eventually left to starve to death. Elizabeth does not leave this room but continues to pay for her crime.

Michael is a man in his mid 30's; he silently stands in the shadows of the cellar, tall and slim, gaunt looking face and piercing eyes. He does not say a lot just stares to intimidate. He came to live in the cellar after his body was brought here from the overflow of the morgue.

Tom and Ben are another two souls that like to make their presence known; they have been picked up by the SLS equipment as it maps out their energy in room 7. Ben being the younger more playful energy and Tom the more negative, they died from an accident involving a cart and horse centuries ago. They were caught on a live feed performing for the camera.

Joseph the barrel boy is another spirit who passed in his prime. When communicating on the Ouija board, he said he was 18 years old when he died after falling into the delivery hatch with barrels of beer and wine crashing down on top of him, breaking his neck. He is only too happy to share the sensations he felt in his final death throes.

Susie's attachment, well now Slender/Shadow man has gone he

is proving to be a force to be reckoned with. He shows up on the SLS camera as a stick figure and grows in size which shows him as huge, you can see him going in and out of Susie. He is oppressive, negative, has a leering grin, dark black eyes, and thick set, tall and very intimidating, often doing obscene and suggestive behaviour in front of the camera. He does not have a name at this moment, not one he wishes to share; he likes to make you feel as uncomfortable as possible to intimidate those who are faint hearted.

*Maureen has come through numerous times on various ghost hunting equipment including on the Ouija boards, EVP, voice boxes and of course through many mediums and guest asking for help. She went missing from the Littlehampton area in the 1960's and now supposedly is behind the wall in the cellar, a good time girl who fell for the wrong man, perhaps. Was she just a play thing of the elite from the Gentlemen's Club who overheard one too many conversations? Did she know too much? Was a game of Russian roulette supposed to scare her but went horribly wrong with one bullet too many? The sound of a gunshot can be heard deep down, down in the cellar in the stillness of the night, is that what took her or was it something more sinister? Will we ever find out...? So many questions with so few answers!

There are many children in The Dolphin, through Ouija and the use of other ghost hunting equipment and trigger objects they have shown themselves. There is a constant flow of children's energies within the rooms, cellars and the garden. From pandemics, paedophilia, work house, orphanages, etc. Children were exploited over the centuries with little regard for their general well being. Also the cellar being the perfect place for the overspill of the morgue, the children came with their bodies and then stayed; perhaps they feel safety in numbers. The amount changes constantly as more are drawn to this portal of light, finding sanctuary perhaps within the dimension between the earth plane and the spirit world.

Transient spirit are souls that are floating around as apparitions, some people believe they are also recognisable as orbs, a thick density, white sphere of light with a darker edge which can come in different colours. They are drawn to The Dolphin by the portal of light especially when we are working within the circle. They make themselves known by interacting, sometimes they are just not ready to cross over but when they are we cross them back into the light. There are just far too many to mention, the above gives you an indication of the diversity of the souls that haunt these walls.

As I complete the final editing of this book a new energy has arrived at The Dolphin, very negative with a darkness that taunts Ellie. William has all but disappeared into the shadows and Susie's attachment stays in the hotel section, this one loiters in the bar...I can feel a sequel coming on... watch this space!

*Name has been changed.

CHAPTER 13

The L.I.G.H.T Paranormal Team...

Ghost Hunters And Anything Else Dodgy And Odd...

E llie has been interested in the paranormal for as long as she can remember, not just ghost hunting. UFO's especially was her main interest. Ellie and her brother used to go out when she was 14 years old looking for UFOs and documenting everything they saw that was unexplainable. They then started to go into the woods looking for ghosts, unusual happenings, and anything supernatural.

In her mid 20's Ellie took her hobby seriously, making little films of their experiences, they actually made a remake of the Blair Witch Project. The hands of fate then brought Ellie to The Dolphin, what better prize for someone who has had a lifetime of interest in the paranormal and the survival of life after death, to end up in a haunted hotel!

In 2006 Ellie formed L.I.G.H.T, which stands for Littlehampton Investigative Ghost Hunting Team, with Mark Green, Brenda and Elaine Rosier, a superb medium who Ellie first met when she did a buffet for her at The Dolphin. Elaine went up to Ellie and said, "Did you know there was a young woman in the loo rolling pastry?" After thinking that this lady had lost her marbles, Elaine explained that she was in fact a medium. Elaine was talking about Jane! Ellie had the biggest 'gob', her words, became the leader of the group and started to organise ghost hunts in woods, private houses and helping people in trouble with spiritual activity. Elaine is also a rescue medium so she helps trapped spirits to go into the light back to the spirit realm. They would also do about 5 ghost hunts a year in The Dolphin, but as the activity increased so did the demand for the hunts.

By this time some members had gone by the wayside, Ellie, Mark, Ken Williams and I are now part of The L.I.G.H.T Paranormal Team conducting the ghost hunts at The Dolphin and various other places. We are all spiritual and empathic, but as investigators we work as a team to prove life after death, debunking anything that does not ring true. When something becomes unexplainable we use our abilities within the team to validate what the others are feeling. Even though Ellie is a hardened investigator with over 25 years of experience, things still make her jump and she is often seen running in the opposite direction.

Every ghost hunter and paranormal group needs technical back up including batteries fully charged and plentiful. One of the things spirit love to do is sabotage, they drain your equipment and use the energy to communicate with us, which is why you can feel drained with an altercation with a spirit, especially ghost hunts, they thrive on our energy. It is also why when you go on hunts you need loads of chocolate and sugar-filled treats to give you a sugar rush to replenish your energy. Our cache of equipment includes K2 meters, EVP voice recorders, spirit box, SLS camera mapping, EMF for registering electromagnetic activity, Rem Pod, cat balls, blue and red torches for transfiguration, heat-sensing guns, sensor bear as a trigger object for children, a spinning Ouija which works on spiritual energy, also the traditional Ouija boards. Although we find the best bit of equipment is us, we are prepared for the slightest of movement from any Casper's, friendly or not!

Facebook live feeds have allowed us to share the experiences of our ghost hunts and have interaction from others interested in the paranormal. Ellie is an experienced and truly gifted investigator who seems to have the ability to draw the spirits out, not always in a conventional way but gets the job done. The spirits are drawn to her so engage and interact fully which at times can result in Ellie running in the opposite direction. Charming, witty, and passionate Ellie is a force to be reckoned with and the evidence she has collected over many ghost hunts has been spell-binding. It is interesting to see comments on the feeds with people's thoughts, feelings, emotions, and foresight of what they can also see and feel. Spiritual intuition is in all of us at different degrees; how we develop it is down to us. It also shows if people are picking up on the same phenomenon at the same time as us. It validates our collective evidence and proves that there is something about this spiritual mythos that is becoming too evident to be ignored. Using Ellie's wealth of experience in the supernatural and magikal realms and being a white witch, she has reopened Pillywiggins, which means a healing flower fairy. Very much like Ellie, Pillywiggins has a dark edge; the shop sells everything to do with spirituality and can be found on Facebook.

As the demand for ghost hunts increases, we will continue to explore other possibilities into the spirit realm. We have seen, heard, and been a part of too many experiences that have left us with many questions that still need to be answered. Of course, there will always be ridicule from people who do not have an open mind, there are those that are quick to judge and think the evidence is doctored or staged, we have far too much integrity for that. Or who believe when you're dead that's it! For us, that is not the case it would taint what we all truly believe, when our bodies die our essence still lives on. Like buying a car really, when our car is knackered we jump into another one and are once again free to go on a journey!

CHAPTER 14

The Most Haunted Experience

Friday the 19th of October 2019 was the first of many weekends to come with the team from the Most Haunted Experience, a splinter group from the TV programme Most Haunted. Together, Ellie, Mark Green, and I worked within the group who had come to The Dolphin Hotel to experience the shenanigans of the spirits that dwell within, they were certainly not disappointed. After the safety briefing and an appearance by Fred Batt from the Most Haunted, we were split off into three groups. Ellie and Mark joined the other two groups, while I joined Andrew and Seth Rogoff-Johnson on the first trip up to room 7 with a bunch of ghost hunters, and boy were those spirits waiting for us! Armed with K2, EMF detectors, heat sensors, EVP electronic voice recorders, RF radio frequency detectors, Rem Pod which makes a loud noise and shows a red light when the temperature drops 5c, also if something touches the antenna other lights will start flashing too. It produces its own electromagnetic field making it easier for a spirit to communicate.

Even the corridor leading to room 7 is like walking into a refrigerator regardless of the weather, with room 7 being the freezer section. Crowding into the room and turning the lights off, with the cat balls strategically placed in the doll's house, child's crib, and on the rocking horse. K2 sensors at the ready in the slightly shaking hands of the guest hunters, we waited, breath held and not a sound to be heard. After a few minutes Seth, Andrew, and I were calling out for the spirits to come forward and show themselves, to give us signs that they were there. The braver guests amongst us, after a few hesitant squeaks, started joining in too. In the darkness of the room, the coolness was apparent as the Rem Pod beeped to the ever descending temperature, breath steam coming from our mouth as we breathed silently in anticipation. The flashing balls burst into life from the child's crib, gasps sounded in the darkness. We then asked questions and the ball flashed in response, intelligent energy wanted to be acknowledged. No one was touching the crib, even though the room was dark the light from the gadgets allowed us to see the silhouettes of where people were sitting and standing within the room, you have to touch the ball for it to flash, so who touched it? Or should I say WHAT? Some of the K2's had gone from the stable green colour and were now flashing up through the scales to red. The meters that were placed in different areas of the room, being held, placed on the floor, by our 'beloved' Susie in her high chair and the doll's house was all reading green. No one touched, moved, or even breathed on them when they started changing colour. Any possible electrical currents that may have set it off like walkie-talkies, cell phones, video cameras, electrical cables, in fact anything that may cause an RF, radiofrequency, had been debunked. Ellie had also done baseline tests on the morning of the hunt. As previously mentioned, K2s pick up on electromagnetic fields, ideally, they need to be used in conjunction with the other specialised ghost hunting equipment, this is to confirm spiritual activity because of the super sensitivity to the electro fields.

By now the guests were experiencing coldness around the legs; this normally happens when the children are about, tightness in the chest, muzzy or painful heads, and mixed emotions. Not wanting to be outdone, the ball on the rocking horse started flashing along with the one in the dolls' house, such an illuminating sight in the darkness of the room. No one had moved or were anywhere near the balls and believe me before we had even started, Seth and Andrew had tested them and even though they were sensitive they did not light up easily.

Knowing and having seen and experienced the delights of room 7, I could not have been happier that the children had come out to play, especially as this was the first time the Most Haunted Experience had visited The Dolphin. Being a medium I could see them and hear their laughter from how their interaction was affecting the ghost hunters within the room.

At this point, Seth being lit by a beam of a torch knelt and started banging on the floor while asking the spirits to copy him. With each rap a response would follow, first of all on the walls, then the ceiling, and eventually the floor shook with each bang beneath our feet. This was more evidence that there was an intelligent energy responding to us. Now I am sure that at this point one or two of you may be thinking someone living obviously was playing with us especially those of you who are sceptic. However, there was no one in the part of the hotel we were in, you would have to drink a lot of red bulls to even remotely lift off the ground let alone reach the outside wall of room 7, on the third floor! Situated at the end of a very long corridor with no access other than the door we walked through. No one was below the room as it is used for storing furniture and had not been opened for years; the only person with a key was Ellie who was on the ghost hunt in the cellar. We were all close enough to each other to know if anyone even silently hiccupped, let alone move within striking distance of the wall, floor, or ceiling.

Following on from the bangs, the sound of a barrel rolling could be heard. Now Fredrick, as mentioned before, was believed to be the old blacksmith come cooper who made barrels in the barn that used to be part of The Dolphin. The distinct sound of a barrel being rolled across the ceiling could be heard bearing in mind that there is no floor in the attic only wooden joists that you have to step over. Any barrel rolling by someone with a pulse in the attic would end up crashing through the ceiling!

As the bangs began to become less intense, the resident small Ouija board table came out to play from the corner of the room. Just to reiterate this is only for experienced users, the table is blessed for each session and worked with only love and light, strictly no alcohol is allowed, and then closed down safely after each use. I sat at the table to get the energy going as this is something I often do as a medium, then swapped places with a guest on the hunt. As they placed their fingers on the glass it started to move. Fingers have to be light on the glass so it can fly across the table, if anyone tries to push it you can feel it and if anyone wanted to play around giving false readings they would soon be found out. The people sitting at the table are constantly changed so everyone gets to experience the energy in a safe environment; due to working with the spirit it can be very draining on the individuals taking part. By changing the guests frequently it maintains the energy needed to get results. One spirit who never passes up the opportunity to entertain the guest and plead his innocence is William, and he certainly did not disappoint! He answered a series of questions asked by us all until he started getting playful, he then kept moving the glass round and round, when I shouted out STOP in a firm voice it was enough to have him shaking in his boots, hypothetically speaking, the glass then stopped dead. He does not like strong women and after I spent a weekend with William, now that's another story within the book in chapter 16, and having the ability to cross him over, he behaves.

On this occasion, surprisingly he admitted he had murdered Jane and was remorseful, did he mean it? Well, you never know with William, sneaky little bugger!

Bringing the table session to a close we went off to room 1, we all crowded in and sat in the darkness with the equipment placed in various locations. Going through the routine of asking the questions, the temperature again started to drop. The balls on the floor started flashing and the K2's again flashed off the scale. Then something happened that I had not experienced before and after speaking to Ellie, she had not been aware of either. Sitting in the darkness we heard furniture being moved around in room 2, directly next door. There were banging and scraping sounds and as we leaned against the door and wall to listen further, there was no doubt it was coming from inside.

The connecting door was locked and when Seth checked the main door the keys were no longer in the lock. They are always left there due to the number of ghost hunts we do, I mean who would want to stay in there.... right!? When they were eventually found in the bar area, bearing in mind no one had left the room, everyone was accounted for within the groups at all times and no one admitted taking them out of the door. Ellie opened up the room and everything was in the same place and no one was inside, your guess is as good as mine.... You'd need a suitcase full of underwear just for one night to stay in that room!

Peter Balsamino, the team leader of The Most Haunted Experience had summoned our group to the bar to listen to what he had recorded on his phone. Intelligent whistling could be heard, Peter asked the spirit to copy the tune he was whistling and the spirit happily complied. There was nowhere or no one the sound could have come from, it was as clear as day. This was witnessed by at least 30 people. Ironically, since that night the whistling is constantly heard in the bar, and not just when people are around, you can walk into the bar and hear it before you have even reached the area it generally comes from. On the next hunt, at the end of November, a music box was clearly heard playing as 35 people stood in the bar listening, with no idea where it was coming from, nothing at all was in the bar that could have made that sound. The whole of The Most Haunted Experience team including Fred, Peter, his wife Carly, Andrew, Seth, Ellie, Mark, and I, along with all the guests stood and listened to the beautiful sound of the music box as it echoed around the bar. As ghost hunters it is about debunking, finding explanations as to whom, where, and why but there was just no answer. Perhaps this music was caught in a time warp of energy playing over and over again, we were just fortunate enough to all be in the right place at the right time or maybe just a playful spirit with an aptitude for music, who knows?....

Being a medium you can be regarded as a con merchant or away with the fairies amongst other things, so validating spirits exist is essential by people who are not, too many are closed off to the possibilities and are quick to judge and dismiss. To stand side by side with sceptics who could not explain what was happening, allowing them to open their minds to the possibilities, gives people like me a chance. Of course, there are charlatans; you will find them in every profession. However, there are more and more people coming to light like me showing that actually there just maybe something more to the paranormal. Rather than having a black and white thought process, by opening up to the grey areas, it gives more possibilities for things to show themselves. There is a saying, 'to a believer no evidence is needed, to a sceptic no evidence is enough!'

From there our group went to the cellar, after the experience in the bar the chances of finding anything remotely as interesting seemed a little futile, again The Dolphin did not disappoint.

Walking into the darkness of the cellar you can feel the heaviness in the air, the Angel table as I like to call it rather than Ouija, which I use for my private teaching, was situated in the middle of the cellar. Turning to the left we ushered the group down to where the barrels are brought down from the street above. Standing in the darkness, which heightens the senses, listening in silence the group started feeling as if they were leaning forward towards the hatch. Some experienced dizziness, nausea, tingling in the legs, pain on one side of the head, and restrictions with breathing. The sensations felt are from the spirit who resides in the cellar called Joseph, who has been mentioned earlier in the book, he fell to his death through the hatch breaking his neck while delivering barrels.

Next, we went into the small room where the compressor sits called the Safe Cellar by Ellie, in this area small stones amongst other things are chucked at anyone standing in there. The group gathered inside while Andrew and I stood in the doorway, a couple of stones came from out of the darkness into the group. The room is too small for anyone to be hiding in the shadows, it is about 12 ft long and 3 feet wide, there is shelving at the end with a small side where the compressor sits on. At this point, the compressor blasted out some air shocking everyone to turn tail and run to the door where Andrew and I were standing. Nothing spooky about that right?... Except when we all gathered together at the end of the night to discuss our evidence and relaying the events of the evening, we found out from Ellie that the compressor had not worked for a week and was missing a part that had been sent away to be replaced!

It was during one of The Most Haunted Experience that the event with the gas bottles happened... just a reminder... When you walk into the cellar on the left-hand side is a stack of large gas bottles that are held in place by two wooden blocks wedged to stop them from rolling. While investigating at the barrel hatch the gas bottles came crashing down, no one was in this area! We went to see what had happened and the blocks were found away from the gas bottles in the centre of the room. If we had any doubt that perhaps they were not stacked properly, this immediately went when the same thing happened again. We had put the bottles back with the wedges firmly in place to continue with the investigation checked by the whole group. Now gas is not something you mess with when you are alive, when your dead, well the dynamics change, you cannot lose what you have not got.

Finishing off with a session on the table the spirits told us their tales along with messages from loved ones for people in the group.

After the session in the cellar, 8 guests and I went back to room 7 just to finish off the evening. The bangs were deafening, it sounded like running in the attic, thuds, tapping, and barrels rolling, Slender man had been pretty quiet earlier in the evening and it seemed as if he was waiting to perform in the finale! Just before leaving room 7 for the night and doing the usual checks, I found the doll's house furniture had been turned upside down.

At the start of the evening, it was all the right way up; no one was left alone in the room to have tampered with the house and its contents.

An amazing night was had by all who were so enthralled with the spooky going on that The Dolphin Hotel was chosen as the No.1 most haunted location in 2019 by The Most Haunted Experience public vote.

CHAPTER 15

Haunted Houses Team-
Dare to be scared

Another fabulous night of ghost hunting mania was with the Haunted Houses Team, they have a massive following on Facebook and YouTube, and have vast experience with many ghost hunts under their belts. They came to The Dolphin Hotel on the 30th of November 2019, this time there was no guests just the team; Adam Bodek-Randle, Nickie Davies, Kate Miller, Ry Clark, Chris Evan, Ellie and I, this was their investigation and we just tagged along.

Of course, the obvious place we were going to start in was room 7. Ghost hunting equipment at the ready including K2, EMF detectors, heat sensors, EVP voice recorders, RF detectors, cat balls, and a REM Pod, we were gadget armed and good to go.

At this time the hostile spirit Ellie and Mark had brought back from Binstead wood in August 2019 was still there, the dark energy of Slender man was waiting in the shadows. He made his presence known as soon as we walked into the room. Standing in the left-hand corner he instantly took a dislike to Nick; William was also waiting in the wings to have his say.

Placing the REM Pod in the middle of the floor, we all sat in various places within the room, Kate and Chris sitting on the settee to the right when you enter. Adam sat in the armchair by the window, Ry sat to the left of the rocking horse, with Nick beside her. I sat next to Susie in her high chair and Ellie stood in front of the doll's house to my right by the door. Sitting in the darkness with the lights of the REM Pod silhouetting us the group started asking for signs that spirit was present. Adam who has mediumistic capabilities told us he could see a cat by the REM Pod, just at that point, the lights started flashing showing movement beside it and the sound went off indicating the drop in temperature. Both Adam and Ry felt the coldness start at their legs, Kate and Chris joined in feeling the same sensation. There appeared to be shadows around the door area, at this point Adam said he could feel two children sitting in front of him, he believed he could see a young girl leaning on the high chair with Susie in it.

Being just an observer rather than using my abilities, it was brilliant for me that someone else could see what I see, it also means I won't be going alone into a straight jacket! The children thought Adam was funny which I relayed and were drawn to him. It was not until afterward that Adam mentioned he was also a school teacher which made perfect sense. The children were comfortable around him so easily showed themselves to such a lovely, friendly person.

It was now time to bring out the Ouija table which had been blessed with holy water and opened with protection from the Lord's Prayer. Adam, Kate, Ry, Chris, and Nick sat around it, placing their fingers on the glass it instantly burst into life slowly at first until it started giving stronger and more precise movements. William came though eager to express his dislike for Nick, being a strong male and leader of the group, and also Adam by spelling out he was a sinner for being part of the LGBTQ community. William with the help of Slender man tried to stir up fear within the group by moving the glass randomly and revealing facts about the team, even attempting to spell out the fictional name of Zozo! (Zozo is supposedly a demonic force that comes through on the Ouija board to create fear and confusion with the inexperienced) William and Slender man were working together as they took over the board. Who would have thought two bad boys would be partners in crime! They would not allow any further intelligent communication just to show their dominance. I am sure I heard a sigh of disappointment from our naughty spiritual friends because the team did not go running for their lives, in fact, we continued with the hunt.

At this point, Nick and Adam headed off to room 2, whilst the rest of us continued in room 7. Kate and Ry began asking a series of questions where the spirit was keen to respond with loud bangs and copying the sounds being made by Kate. As we were sitting in the room we heard a loud bang from outside in the corridor and two voices talking as if Nick and Adam were retuning. Ellie went out into the corridor and walked back to the fire door which is a good 200 meters from room 7, no one was there and no one was in any of the other rooms. Ten minutes later when Nick and Adam returned, we asked them if they had been speaking in the corridor earlier and when they shook their heads, the gulps were deafening!

At the same time that we had heard the noises, Nick and Adam had gone into room 2 and the K2's had started to flash. Moving on to room 1 to continue the investigation which is directly next door, they both heard footsteps coming down the stairs that are situated outside room 2. The door opened up and someone walked inside, they then heard movement from within room 2. Adam went to check, on opening up the door no one was there!

Both groups experienced noises at the same time in different locations of the hotel which was on lockdown, with no one else in the building. A late night rendezvous of past lovers known to haunt the corridors of The Dolphin? Residual energy caught on a time loop to continually play a moment in time? The only ones that knew were the ones making the noise, who that was... your guess is as good as mine!

Leaving Adam and Nick to do a live feed the rest of us went to room 2. Walking into the room the temperature, as usual, would make a penguin feel right at home. Ellie was conducting a live feed for The Haunted Dolphin Hotel Facebook page. We put 5 K2 meters on the bed and I started recording an EVP session while Ellie and Kate asked a series of questions. Ellie asked, "If the spirit had died here?" A very clear and audible disembodied voice responded 'Yes', which was also caught on the live feed. The K2 meters by now were all flashing from green to red at different points on the bed. The bed had previously been checked that there was nothing that could affect the K2's, even the recording device. Goosebumps had goose bumps; the sensations of feeling watched were very apparent and slightly uncomfortable even for the experienced ghost hunters.

Adam and Nick rejoined us in room 2; they informed us that when we had left room 7 there were more loud bangs. Every time Dolly's name was mentioned the K2's started going over into the red, all of which was captured on the Haunted Houses live feed. Was Dolly communicating with them or William pretending to be an innocent child? The intriguing thing was when both Kate and Nick were doing a series of knocks in a certain pattern, intelligent responses were given by something, William or otherwise? Remember this room is three stories up, only one corridor to get to it, one independent attic with no one hiding in the eaves, and the room next to it locked. So for all you doubting Debbie's thinking someone was hiding doing the knocks in an old building, guess you come down and find out for yourselves.

Once we had updated Adam and Nick on the activity in room 2, we carried out a series of tests with the K2 moving them around the bed, and still, they were lighting up like Blackpool illuminations. The spirits communicated to the questions that were asked by using the lights of the K2. The sensations of tightness in the chest, pressure around the throat, and the feeling of being watched with something standing up close and personal could all be felt. When the communication from the spirit was a resounding 'Yes' after the question, "Did you die here?"....Well, the clues were there!

Leaving Adam and Nick in room 2 we went down to the back cellar known as the Coffin Room which used to run underneath the pub and be joined to the main cellar, it is now two small rooms joined by a doorway with narrow steps leading down. In one room there is a boiler and a massive chimney breast where you can hear voices whispering and chattering; in the other is an old coal shoot and an old copper boiler which is no longer in use, four chairs and a table with an Ouija board placed upon it. Information from the Ouija and a ghostly apparition seen by many, suggest a spirit of a little boy called Thomas, he allegedly helped with the coal deliveries and died after falling down the shoot and was suffocated from the dust and the weight of the coal. He is often seen covered in black dust and the smell of coal seems to intensify when he is around. Kate, Ellie, Ry, Chris and I were sitting in the darkness when tiny stones started hitting us and falling to the ground, was this the coal boy or another little girl called Elizabeth who allegedly was locked in the cellar for stealing bread and left to die? Kate had the feeling a very negative spirit was behind her and standing up close and personal. This is one of the resident spirits who is a large, bald chap who smells of sweat and alcohol and loves the ladies, especially their bottoms, he likes to intimidate. He loves it when you show fear he feeds off your emotions. With gentle reassurance for Kate not to show fear and a flea in his spiritual ear, the chancer Dave left Kate alone. Being able to see, hear, sense, taste, and smell I am not intimidated, he was not the most handsome of chaps and was a little too fond of the whisky. Again the K2's were flashing away like Christmas tree lights and a temperature drop that made an iceberg feel like a toasted marshmallow. Kate commented afterward that she had never felt such fear as she had done whilst in the Coffin Room cellar with this intensive low vibration of energy. An experienced investigator she is usually very guarded and calm but it was clear to see that this event had shaken her to the core.

After regrouping and checking on evidence gathered, Ry had to return home and Ellie went into her flat to check on her dogs, the rest of us went down to the front cellar where bodies were stored when the morgue was full. Putting the REM Pod at the doorway between the large cellar and the passageway that leads to the barrel hatch, we sat around the Ouija table. Both Adam and I exclaimed to the rest of the group that we could see a little boy standing by the REM Pod, as we spoke the words, the REM Pod burst into life with a loud, ear-piercing beep. The lights flashed as if someone was touching it and another loud bleep as the temperature dropped. As we were looking into the darkness a loud bang came from the hatchway which echoed around the cellar. Believe me, it was loud! The video that captures the sound did not do it justice. I must admit I did laugh at their response, scared was an understatement! If I had been a bit more of a Steven Spielberg I would have captured their facial reactions as I was videoing at the time. Grouping together the team tentatively went to explore where the sound had come from, all the doors were securely shut, there was no evidence of where it had come from, or who or what had made it! There was definitely no one living in the cellar as the only things with a pulse were huddled together in a narrow passageway looking a tad pale!

Standing together calling out into the shadows for some kind of response, a white cable hung across the ceiling started to move as if on command. When questions were asked it would flick upwards as if in answer, the spirits were only too happy to show themselves in a way where they could communicate with the living. All of which was filmed for a live feed of Haunted Houses. At one stage I actually was not sure whose heart was beating the loudest was it the Haunted Houses team or the heart of The Dolphin...?

Splitting into two groups again, Kate and Nick went back to room 7, while Adam, Chris, and I stayed in the cellar. Whilst in the cellar again, the K2's were going off the scale, both Adam and I could see an apparition of a little boy in shorts with a short, scruffy bowler hair cut standing next to the old dumbwaiter lift, it is fenced off with 'Do not enter' as it has been condemned. I encouraged the boy to play with a ball and promptly the REM Pod burst into life, all the colours were flashing in response to my voice as the little boy was only too happy to play, especially with the sounds and pretty colours a reward for his interaction.

While in the cellar we kept hearing a ball bouncing down the stone stairs, they lead down from the bar to the door that opens up into the cellar where we were sitting. On opening the door, no one was there and not a ball to be seen, the bar was also empty! The activity was just amazing, perhaps Tommy, the little boy who always bounces his ball in different parts of the hotel, wanted to join in with the ghost hunt.

The Dolphin did not disappoint and the team was in awe with what they had seen and heard throughout the evening. To finish it off as we returned to the bar area we could hear whistling from cabin boy Dickie, a playful tune enchanting to hear.

Adam, Nick, Kate, Chris, and I started whistling and Dickie happily responded, not only behind the bar but around the bar and down by the pool table. The whistling echoed hauntingly, eerie but truly wonderful. There was nothing that could have made this sound as everything had been debunked. Every time we have a ghost hunt Dickie is only too happy to entertain.

By this time Nick said, "I am done, I have been to over 1500 ghost hunts and this is easily one of the most haunted places I have ever been to!"

As I waved them goodbye with their promise of returning soon, I had so much pride in the old girl Dolly. The Dolphin is just like an onion with each layer peeled the stronger the essence and better the taste. It is so easy to understand why Ellie is so passionate about her and the secrets she is slowly showing to the world. I am finding myself becoming more captivated every day and I feel immense joy being among the spirits of the long since dead, hearing their chatter with secrets revealed. Even though I do not live at The Dolphin I feel like it is my second home.

CHAPTER 16

Something is intriguing about orbs

As ghost hunters, we look for anything that may indicate signs of spirits, often looking for light anomalies or balls of energy that appear in photographs or to the naked eye, these are often called orbs. They can appear as flat, cloudy disks in photos, some may have colour tinting in them, or they may have a mottled appearance. Some people believe they see faces or Angels in orbs, however, some sceptics believe this is a trick of the mind called Pareidolia. This is when the mind seeks to see the familiar shapes in random patterns if in doubt ask others for their thoughts. Orbs caught on videos and seen with the naked eye often look 3-dimensional and can appear to be lit like a bulb of a flashlight. It is important to consider many factors before identifying the object as a ghost orb. There has been much controversy about orbs, many sceptics saying they are dust particles, raindrops, snowflakes, pollen, insects, etc. If you have checked your environment and the conditions before taking the photos and know there are no other reasons why you have seen or captured an orb, then rest assured that is what it is. Dust particles are blamed on most film captures, and the way to identify them is that the particles float tending to go in one way with irregular edges. Orbs are generally a circular globe and follow a directional path with the ability to change direction and can have different colours. Of course, the need to check it is not some kind of insect is important to enable you to debunk any questionability. These balls of light can come in a range of sizes and illumination, with some barely visible, others brightly glowing and also the flashing variety. There can be a thick line on the outer edge and a face can sometimes be visible. Now before you get too excited about what you may have captured on film or seen, keep in mind seeing an orb does not necessarily signify that a spirit is nearby.

Many feel that a true ghost orb is one of a spiritual nature. Are these spirits of the dead who are perhaps trapped on the earth plane? Or spirits of their loved ones who have crossed over and this is the form they have taken to show their presence? Some people believe that this is so for both and that it is the first sign of a manifestation of a spirit. There are others who believe these spheres are actually many spirits all combined within the various lights that form an orb. Reckon they would be a bit squashed if that is the case! Still, others believe that while these orbs are spirits, they are not actually 'human' and have never had a body preferring to believe they are elemental and that they are evidence of the spiritual side of nature. The sceptics believe it is a load of rubbish. Their loss I say, for the thought of a loved one showing themselves to their families left behind on the earth plane, can give such a sense of comfort.

There are many ideas associated with the shape of an orb and light anomalies and how they can be identified as a spirit or a ghost. It can be hard to identify things since you are dealing with the spirit world but from my belief and the knowledge I have gained from my guides, this is MY understanding as to why spirit may show themselves as a circle of light:

- A circle of light or orb is easier to travel as it has no edges, just look at a bubble.
- The circle encloses around the spirit in a complete unit.
- Being a circle, if there is more than one inside then no one has the uncomfortable bit. Just looking at all options...
- The circle is a universal symbol representing eternity, there is no end, the life span of forever for the soul which continually evolves.
- The circle is associated with nature, such as the moon and the sun.

Orbs and light anomalies can also show themselves as distorted circles, oblong, having a tail, and as we found out on a ghost hunt at The Dolphin by a spirit who really wanted to get our attention. It formed a solid sideways figure of 8, this also means limitless or eternity. This can be found on the live feed of The Haunted Dolphin Hotel when Mark went into the loft. After all orbs and light anomalies are energy. The stills can also be found in the photograph section.

Orbs can be singular, pulsating; this is a bright orb that appears to vibrate which may actually hold an intelligent, spiritual life force. Contrails; these are very common as they leave a trail as they move across the room. Orbs can also produce their light source, be mindful of flashes from cameras causing reflections. The naked eye is the best evidence of all.

Orbs do not come with an instruction manual so there are not any clear criteria for determining whether an orb is spiritual by nature. However, if you have carefully evaluated the conditions, what you saw, and the way the orb appears or moves, you may get a better idea of its cause, also by debunking any other reason as to why you may have captured what you think is an orb or light anomalies then the chances are you have captured exactly that.

Orbs cause the biggest debate in the paranormal circles, I have seen too many amazing sights involving orbs and light anomalies to ever question that they exist.

While in the New Forest in 2015, I lost my beloved white German shepherd Mylo. When we were leaving the vets after saying our goodbyes to Mylo, my son Callum and I opened the back door of the car and told Mylo to get in. Through our belief in spiritualism, we felt Mylo's energy force would come with us. We drove back to the caravan site where we were staying and opened up the back door of the car again, we called out Mylo as we went into the caravan where our 10-week old kitten Mylee was waiting for us. As soon as we entered the caravan the temperature dropped rapidly, bearing in mind it was the 10th of August and boiling outside which can make a caravan warm.

Mylee's hair was standing on end; I told Callum to quickly sit on the bed with Mylee by his side and took a photo. Besides Callum's head was an orb in the shape of a white German shepherd, too coincidental to be dismissed especially how Mylee was behaving and the coldness of the caravan. We knew he was there letting us know he had not left our side and giving reassurance at such a traumatic time that he would always be there. The photograph can be found at the back of the book which I have done in black and white to emphasis the orb which is undeniably the head of a white dog.

The different colours of orbs are related to their energy, there are many theories about what different orb colours mean, and can vary depending on different beliefs. In some cases, people think colours may have no meaning at all, or it may be how a spirit is trying to communicate with colour to represents their emotions and something important, or it may be relevant to the onlooker.

Below you will find MY interpretation based on my spiritual beliefs and understanding and NOT based on scientific fact.

Clear orbs: The spirit may be trying to communicate with you and to let the living know that some kind of significant event happened in the location where they are, sometimes called a crisis apparition. The spirit may also be letting you know it needs help to move on.

Silver orbs: Are messengers associated with spirituality and connection with a higher source.

Golden orbs: Angelic energy full of unconditional love, guardian Angels are watching over you.

White orbs: A spirit is present to offer protection to visitors, family members, and loved ones, white energy is typically perceived as highly positive in nature.

Yellow orbs: This is a sign of warning of potential danger not necessarily from the living but from negative spirits.

Violet/Purple orbs: These are showing guidance for spiritual matters and information.

Pink orbs: This is a universal message of love; spiritual love of an ascended master, spirit guide, teacher, or archangel. As well as a more specific love of a deceased family member who comes to you in the form of a spirit orb to say they are still with you. Whoever the message comes from it is full of encouragement, peace, hope, and unconditional love.

Peach orb: Spirit is there to give comfort and compassion when you need it the most.

Red/Orange orbs: Are associated with protection, forgiveness, safety, and security and a sense of belonging. These orbs are a sign that an entity has assumed the role of a protector, to keep watch or a caretaker. While these colors are normally associated with strong emotions, such as anger and passion, this is not the case when it comes to spiritual orbs, unless it is huge and acting in an aggressive manner.

Green orbs: Are healing energies, representing love, and oneness with nature. Some orbs under this realm are nature orbs that contain elemental spirits, they can be light green or transparent, they shine, bob and bounce over nature and along the surface of the water and tend to travel in large groups.

Blue orbs: These come in various shades and are a very calming colour meaning protection, tranquillity, and peace. It is associated with psychic energy, spiritual guidance, and truth.

Grey Smoky orbs: There is an indication of depression, lack of spiritual awareness, fear, or ambivalence; it may indicate the presence of a depressed spiritual entity. An indication of confusion or troubling energies.

Brown/Black orbs: Theses colours are associated with earthbound and lower, spiritual vibrations or heavy energy. Their energies tend to be negative in nature, where you can feel oppressiveness and unsafe. Change in emotions needs to be examined with caution, and if you feel uncomfortable or unsafe, leave the vicinity or if it is in your home sage it thoroughly.

Now some people do not believe in sage, however, years ago it was used to help get rid of the disease, all I would say is do not knock it until you try it. Say the Lord's Prayer while asking any negative energies to leave, opening the windows and doors as you fan the smoke around your home starting at the room furthest away and closing each door behind you. Once it is cleared see for yourself how light your house feels.

The colours of orbs can be vibrant or pale depending on the energy, especially if an orb is that of a deceased person, then the colour is dictated by the aura of the person's soul in its disembodied form. Be mindful of lens flare that can affect the colour of the orbs, it can give you misleading information to the actual colour.

The meaning of orbs is believed to be the true form of spirits or souls. The existence of orbs has evolved into a commonly accepted belief among many paranormal investigators. The size of orbs is considered significant, the bigger the orb is the level of the soul's evolution and how spiritually evolved at the time of death, the smaller the orbs the lower the energy. Some people believe the size of the orb shows the power of emotion, for example, a huge red orb behaving erratically would indicate a very angry spirit or even a demon: A large gold or white orb would be a powerful angelic or divine energy.

Being a spiritualist and medium, the orbs I have experienced at milestones within my life have shown to me beyond doubt that they are signs that spirit is always around us regardless of what others may think. What you believe is entirely up to you, not everything in life is explainable and sometimes the simplest of things that can give you at times the greatest sign, pleasure, and comfort is all that matters.

CHAPTER 17

Thought's anyone?...No,
well here is mine...

The Dolphin Hotel is such an amazing place, I have conducted countless ghost hunts and still I am intrigued, surprised, fascinated, and infatuated with the building. Every time I walk in the door of the hotel my legs become freezing cold as I receive ghostly hugs from the spiritual children that dwell in The Dolphin. For me, it has been an incredible experience learning about its quirky ways and also of the spirits within. People tend to think that spirit can be trapped in a building, whether it is the fact that The Dolphin is part of my life now and I return each week to do the circle, that it allows the spirits to have a bit of freedom as many times when I have left The Dolphin, spirit, usually children come home with me. They love playing with my cats who are used to the spirits in my house so just go along with it. Due to the ever-revolving portal door, there is a constant stream of spirits coming into The Dolphin; I feel they come home with me because they know I will cross them over when they are ready. I work with spirit 7 days a week; my whole house is a golden portal of light. I often see streams of spirit walking into the walls as it shines like a beacon to help lost souls go back to the spirit realm. I regularly close portals and cleanse houses of negative energy for people who are experiencing spiritual and poltergeist activity, so I feel the spirit's trust in me. I am there to do no harm just to ensure that the light takes over the dark and I feel, in time, this will happen. In the summer of 2019 when I retreated to the New Forest in my 30-year-old caravan for my spiritual growth and healing with my son, cats and guinea pigs, over 20 'adults' and 50 'children' came with me. I should have charged rent! The children returned to The Dolphin at the end of the summer, the adults did not but remain safe in the knowledge that there are many elemental green portals scattered around so when they are ready they can go into the light. As for the children they are happy where they are right now and when the time is right I will cross them over too.

I believe everything happens for a reason, I was drawn to The Dolphin and was supposed to meet Ellie. The spirits wanted to be heard and my guides listened to help them, for people to understand The Dolphin and hopefully to give them peace. They love to interact when investigators and mediums come in. Of course, there will be negatives and mischievous energies that want to mess with the living, and the dark forces will always be at work, but I will make sure that the mediums in training and I will always be on hand to ensure the spirits of The Dolphin are heard and protected, even William!

When I first started going to The Dolphin, William would try to intimidate me by stepping into my aura... Not only am I a medium, but I am also a strong woman which he absolutely detests. On a singles night in the summer of 2019, William decided he was coming home with me, without an invite. Spirit can manipulate things and make you feel something when in fact it is completely different. As my back started getting colder and colder, I asked Ellie to check it as it felt like bindweed was spreading through my aura. As much as she tried she could not get it off, William was trying to give the impression he was a frightened little boy spirit called Tommy who I am very fond of, even showing him with his ball under his arm. As the evening was coming to an end, I had to leave and as I was driving home I could hear laughter and looked up into my rearview mirror and there as clear as day was William, bless his little cotton socks! I know I am protected by my guides so knew that this was just an inconvenience. When I got home it was like he was trying to take over with his negative energy, which is when he realised he had bit off more than he could chew. He was like one of those annoying gnats that you just cannot seem to swat. I was lying in bed and I could feel my guides coming forward, the portal in my room started to glow and William was starting to be pulled through it. He was screaming and begging for it to stop, I then gave him an ultimatum, I said, "You go back to The Dolphin, never to step foot in my aura again or be sent up to spirit or out to roam the earth plane without a home." Not a peak was heard from him again until I returned to The Dolphin. As soon as I entered the spirit children gathered round me yelling, 'Get out William, get out of Wendy!' Ellie was so angry with him telling him that The Dolphin was his home. The thought of feeling wanted created a shift change in William, he is still unpredictable, annoying on the Ouija, and loves freaking people out but The Dolphin would not be the same without him. William happily talks about our 'dirty' weekend on the Ouija and I still feel him close but not that close just a respectful, curious close.

I have a little pocket Angel board, or Ouija whatever you wish to call it. I look at it as being like a mobile phone texting function, the difference is a pendulum moves over it and spells out what spirit wish to say. It also confirms what the ghost hunting apparatus is picking up with just a little more detail. It is also fascinating to watch a pendulum swinging in such a controlled manner spelling out messages from the spiritual mouth so to speak.

The photograph and video of the imp are very real, there are dark forces at play but they tend to stay in the shadows, whether it is because when we work in the circle we bring positive energy which keeps the darkness at bay, who knows? Only the dark entities themselves know the answer to that. However, when people come to visit on ghost hunts then it is a very different story, it is like spirit coming alive, hypothetically speaking! They love to interact, make your toes curl, give you goose bumps along with a whole array of sensations to scare the living daylights out of you, and give you the time of your life, that you will never forget. The staff and customers are used to the shenanigans of the mischievous entities. Being voted by The Most Haunted Experience as the No1 most haunted venue by the public shows exactly how active it is, in fact, it has been listed in the top 10 most active places. I would say to anyone who is interested in the paranormal come along, witness for yourself and if you dare to be scared, stay the night.

The outcome of The Dolphin is uncertain, with expensive overheads and a brewery that is not budging in their demands; it is very hard for businesses to survive. Whether the spirits of The Dolphin are trying to help Ellie keep the doors open or are afraid themselves of what might happen, they just keep delivering. The experiences I have witnessed and felt have just been breathtaking, thankfully, not literally. It has helped my senses excel, my understanding of spirit to increase, and know not to write spiritual hauntings off as all bad. While doing a house clearing recently a lady asked me why I give spirit the option of going back to spirit or out into the world? The reason being, fear got them where they are at the moment, by helping, guiding, and trusting in the spirit it is allowing then the chance to not fear but give them hope of a better existence in the spirit realm when they are ready to cross over. After all, when we come onto the earth plane we do not come with an instruction manual and have to find out by our own mistakes and experiences, good and bad, sometimes the spirit is just misunderstood and frightened souls trying to find their way.

Many people are probably wondering why I do not close the portals down. There are a few reasons, when a red portal closes the spirit do not necessarily go to the spirit realm, fear can still leave then earthbound. The doorway closing can leave a lot of restless spirits to go out into the world leaving them 'homeless' and looking for some other place to reside. I am sure the people living in Littlehampton do not want a friendly (sometimes) Casper taking residence in their lounge any time soon. The children feel safe where they are along with the many other souls that live there; we work in The Dolphin to continually cross spirit over which we will continue to do so, by educating the mediums of the circle and other up and coming spiritualists.

The universe is still such a mystery, there are many things that cannot be explained, to some, I probably sound like an absolute nutter, to others, you know exactly where I am coming from. The difference in how you feel about me is whether you are open to possibilities, open to the impossible, and what-ifs. I can guarantee I am of sound mind, many inventors, scientists, and physicists have been ridiculed over the centuries for their inventions and beliefs because they have shown other alternatives. It may not be until death that you will realise the whole truth of the matter but holding on to a what-if attitude may help with the transition when your time comes. In the meantime, I will continue to enjoy my experiences with spirit, helping loved ones communicate through the dimensions and offer to give closure, happiness, and peace where needed.

Many of the spirits that have shown themselves I have tried to trace, but it has been very hard, to say the least. In a past where people have been exploited and death is just an inconvenience and the ones that have been registered are few and far between, hopefully, in this day and age, everyone counts. Many spiritual guests have come in on the tide passing through; young adults, prostitutes, and children were disposable, negative publicity was bad for business. The experiences at The Dolphin have been felt by numerous people on several different occasions. There are many live feeds and documented evidence on The Haunted Dolphin Hotel and The L.I.G.H.T Paranormal Team Facebook page where you can make your own mind up, better still, pop in if you dare to be scared......

The information and photographs have been supplied by Ellie Boiling and I. The front cover was provided by the universe in a freaky lightning display in August 2019 and taken by Ellie, coincidence or not, it obviously knew it would be needed to help tell The Dolphin's tale.

CHAPTER 18

The final goodbye...... or is it?

T he outcome of The Dolphin Hotel now lies in fates hands, times have been hard enough with the smoking laws changing, high leasehold repayments, cheap drinks in other public houses that are not tied to the brewery's charges, rising prices due to taxes and the list goes on. The old Dolly is such an old building that holds so much history, character, and energy, the thought of it having to shut its doors for good is truly devastating.

The biggest threat of all now, a pandemic with the potential to be matched with the Spanish flu of 1918 is now invading the whole world. To save lives the British population is now in lockdown and social distancing as I write this last chapter, with the forecast of many lives being lost. Is this the final nail in the coffin of The Dolphin, after nearly 300 years of history? Well, that will be down to the universe. The chances of it becoming a busy and thriving business once the pandemic has passed with Ellie at its realm, is debatable, being able to sustain a hotel and bar with social distancing and still be able to cover the enormous costs with limited clientele, is daunting. The outcome depends on so many things, hopefully, faith and fate will step in. If the doors do not remain open with Ellie to protect them, know that the spirits will be helped on their way by myself and the mediums within the circles I hold.

Maybe, just maybe I will have more chapters to write in the future.......until then thank you to all the punters who have visited, enjoyed the hospitality, the amazing food, and sampled a tipple at the bar. Those who have loved laughed attended many of the ghost hunts on lives and in person and the guests brave enough to sleep within the walls, especially the ones who made it to the morning! Right now The Dolphin has paused, stopped at a moment in time and the walls now just resonate with the memories of the past if you listen very, very carefully you may even hear the piano playing, the laughter of locals past and present, and glasses chinking in toasts to the future. Ellie is still holding live feeds on Facebook where you can feel the emptiness of what was once a thriving hub of the community. It is now replaced with a quiet soulless space where the spirits are waiting for the energy of the living to bring life back into the dead. The spirits seem to know and come alive when the camera is watching to ensure they are not forgotten, waiting to play their part replaying the echo's of their timeline, while passing the time away. They are waiting for the outcome of their home to see where their destiny lies so they can once again be involved in creating memories in the future history of The Haunted Dolphin hotel. When The Dolphin opens its doors once again for ghost hunts, there will be a queue of paranormal teams wishing to investigate the hauntings within the corridors and foundations of this extraordinary spiritual space. One of the first teams that will come through those doors will be Stabbed in the Back UK events team owned by Steve and Shazzie Jennings; they have shown Ellie such support during this difficult time when Ellie has needed it the most.

We send out love and light to every one of you who has supported Ellie over the last 20 years while she has been the landlady of such a magnificent, landmark in Littlehampton's history, and to the ones who have purchased this book to help the doors stay open. Take care, stay safe, and hopefully when the doors do open without restrictions The Dolphin Hotel will be thriving once again one day soon, until then..............

......do you dare to be scared?

THE HAUNTED DOLPHIN HOTEL

A welcoming haven for not only the living
but also for the spirits of the dead.

Taken in 1887 with how the hotel used to look.

Taken in 1901 The Dolphin advertising one of the first garages in England which was underneath the bar area.

The Most Haunted Experiences prestigious
award which is decided by the public.

THE L.I.G.H.T PARANORMAL
TEAM AND GUESTS
ELLIE BOILING

Ellie has been the landlady for over 20 years and is
the leader of the team. Clairsensient herself Ellie
senses the energies around her rather than sees.

WENDY JACK

Wendy is a clairvoyant and psychic medium who has been a member of the team since May 2019, also the Author of The Haunted Dolphin Hotel. Wendy undertakes demonstrations, spiritualist church services, gives personal readings, and works on behalf of various outlets including TV programmes and magazines giving readings all over the world.

MARK GREEN

Mark is the lead investigator in the team since it started in 2006. Mark is also a medium and attends Wendy's development circles to enhance his abilities. Working as a ghost hunter he combines his spiritual and practical side.

KEN WILLIAMS

Ken Williams is an investigator in the team since 2018. He also is empathic to spirits and has mediumistic tendencies.

Working as a team combining spirituality as well as using practical ghost hunting equipment, it allows us to see things we may not necessarily pick up on.

Having an open mind means anything is possible.

LIVE FEED GHOST HUNTS

Ellie has been doing the ghost hunts while in lockdown with various guests. Our friend Steve Jennings from SIB who has mediumistic abilities joined us on this one; the faces say it all as the spirits were pretty feisty.

Another live ghost hunt with special guest Adam Bodek-Randle from Haunted Houses who is also a medium in training.

TRANSFIGURATION

Mark starting the process of transfiguration as the energy of Slender/Shadow man stepped into his aura. The spirit used ectoplasm to puff out Mark's face to resemble how he would have looked when he was alive.

As Slender/Shadow man's negative energy started to consume Mark his face changed drastically. Shortly after this reaction, Mark was brought out of the transfiguration. Afterwards he started coughing and became ill. It is not for the faint-hearted as the energy attached himself to Mark which we had to get out of his aura.

Experienced ghost hunters only please!

NEWSPAPER ARTICLES

Just a few of the Newspaper articles on the
spooky events at The Dolphin Hotel.

CENSUS

Census were carried out every 10 years, whoever was staying in the hotel on that day was documented. Was it fool-proof? No! I tried tracing Jane Buxey on one of the forms, date of birth 1857, no details were found, and on looking further she was actually born in 1858. However, there was no record of death, marriage, or otherwise. Jane is probably still roaming around without a care in the world at the ripe old age of 162, so handle with care if you see her about! The census for 1931 was lost in a fire while the 1841 census results went missing from Wrexham and later turned up in a bookshop. People were judgemental on the forms too, a 19th Century minister recorded a butcher as a 'cut-throat of pigs' and mothers of illegitimate children as 'whore and man trap' charming! Suffragette Emily Wilding Davidson hid in a cupboard in Parliament on census night and had her address recorded as the Houses of Parliament and in 1841 art-ist JMW Turner rowed a boat into the Thames so he could not be counted as being present at any property. In 2001 religion was included for the first time since 1851; it was amazing that 390,000 people were from the Jedi and Star Wars religion! What about the other 364 days and 9 years you ask? Well, that is free for all, when checking so infrequently it really is not a good way of tracking people, many slipped under the radar. With so many nooks and crannies' in The Dolphin Hotel you could hide a whole army and they wouldn't be detected. If someone did not want to be found they would not be! A couple of coins in the right hand and you do not even exist; paperwork was easy to forge with no DNA, fingerprints, photographs, or electronic id. In those days you could be anybody you wanted to be except the person you actually were. The port was busy with many a traveller coming in on the tide or leaving making it hard to keep track of the comings and goings of people. Pick -pockets, vagabonds, ladies of the night, tinkers, murderers, thieves, high-waymen, and just general all-round dodgy persons would not want their location known, ever watchful of easy pickings they would roam wherever their fortune took them. When The Dolphin Hotel was first built it would have been the classy place to go but over time it became a shabby den of iniquity in days gone by.

Below you will find one of the census forms where Thomas Staples is on. While I was looking at the names of people I found myself visualising how they would have lived and worked in their professions like a snapshot in time.

∧ / Robert Daniel / Tailor / 18 /
Bloomsbury, London / Census

1855 / Thomas Staples /... / Post Office
Directory *

1859 / Abraham Betchley /... / Post Office
Directory *

1861 / Richard Hammond / Head, Licensed
Victualler / 35 / Arundel, Sussex / Census *

MEDIUM SPIRIT ARTIST
DEBBIE DEAN'S DRAWINGS

William

Jane

The murder victim of William if the spirits communication
through mediums, Ouija boards, spirit boxes, K2's, SLS
camera, and countless EVP's are anything to go by.

*Maureen

The lady behind the wall in the cellar if the spirits
are to be believed.

STRUCTURED LIGHT SENSOR CAMERA

the spirits of the Dolphin

The stick figures you see below are created by the cameras built-in infrared invisible grid over the projected view. The grid is made up of over a million tiny dots, these laser dots form a grid that gives the device its name SLS, Structured Light Sensor. The sensors can calculate the distance between the infrared dots for it to build a three-dimensional model. If something moves within its field of view there will be a change of movement within the dots that the camera recognises. The software can highlight human figures in the images it captures detecting limbs and movement, showing them as stickmen.

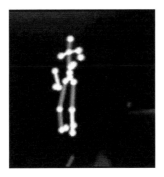

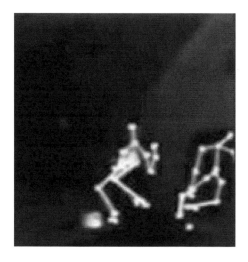

Two spirit children interacting by flashing a ball to command.

This picture shows Susie's attachment standing
over her before he went back into the doll.

ORBS AND LIGHT ANOMALIES

Many orbs were present while using a planchette with a
pen as little Dolly and the spirit children drew hearts.

A white orb appeared beside my son Callum after we had lost Mylo, our white German Shepherd.

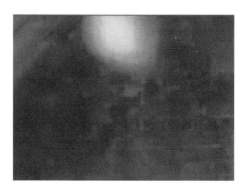

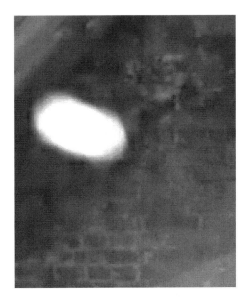

This was an amazing light anomaly caught on video as Mark went into the attic it flew towards him, went past then went back and hovered in front of him. It was NOT a bug! You can see the full video on The Haunted Dolphin Hotel Facebook.

FABULOUSLY SPOOKY PHOTO'S!

... to make your spine tingle
and pacemaker fail

Here are just a few of the captures that can be found on the Facebook page of The Haunted Dolphin Hotel.

This video has gone viral, you can see a lady at the bar with what looks like an imp materialising behind her caught on the CCTV. The video was analysed to make sure it had not been tampered with.

In the ladies toilets where Jane loiters ready to tell anyone who dares to enter 'get out of my kitchen!' With a ghostly shove for those who outstay their welcome! Anyone too vain gets pushed against the glass, so remember ladies beauty is only skin deep, it's what is inside that counts!

A video still from a ghost hunt captures one of the spirit children, a little boy with his head on his knees and his arms around his legs. He was up in the attic when the light anomaly showed up. A negative energy trying to keep the children under control perhaps?

The old nanny captured on a ghost hunt caught on
a time loop as she watches over her wards...?

LITTLE DOLLY

Little Dolly's photograph was found in the secret cupboard in room 7, a lovely little girl who loves to play with the guests. She may not be here in person but her spirit lives on in

The Haunted Dolphin Hotel.

FACEBOOK

Thank you for taking the time to read this tribute to The Dolphin Hotel. Whatever your beliefs whether you are cynical or not I hope you have enjoyed the experiences we have shared.

Please look at The Haunted Dolphin Hotel and The L.I.G.H.T Paranormal Team Facebook pages where you can see countless videos of ghost hunts with spooky moments; Ellie may be screaming, you have been warned!

Captured screenshots, census forms, publications, spirit drawings and so much more, I have only shared a minute selection. If you can why not pop down for a ghost hunt and see for yourself...

...if you dare to be scared....?

INFORMATION REFERENCE

https://thehamillhouse.wordpress.com/2016/11/02/scammers-spiritualism-and-ghosts-the-victorian-obsession-with-the-paranormal/

https://en.wikipedia.org/wiki/Spiritualism

https://www.westsussex.gov.uk/media/1734/littlehampton_eus_report_and_maps.pdf

http://www.bbc.co.uk/history/ancient/romans/

https://www.visionofbritain.org.uk/place/961

https://www.uniquemagazines.co.uk/Love-It-Magazine-

http://www.littlehamptonmuseum.co.uk/

https://www.indiatoday.in/world/asia/story/3-year-old-remembers-past-life-identifies-killer-location-of-body-193650-2014-05-20

https://www.bustle.com/articles/180212-5-creepy-haunted-dolls-who-want-to-play-with-you-forever-and-ever-and-ever

https://www.mosthauntedexperience.com/

http://www.bbc.co.uknewscensus2020eightthingsyouneedtoknow-aboutcensus

https://www.imdb.com/title/tt8865774/ Help! My houses is Haunted 2018 The Dolphin Hotel

WHERE TO FIND US

The Dolphin Hotel/Pub
34, High Street
Littlehampton West Sussex
BN17 5ED
Tel: 01903 715789
Mob: 07803210188
dolphin@dolphin-littlehampton.co.uk
www.dolphin-littlehampton.co.uk

Facebook:
The Haunted Dolphin Hotel
The Dolphin Hotel
The L.I.G.H.T Paranormal Team
Wendy Jack, Clairvoyant and Psychic Medium

ABOUT THE AUTHOR

Wendy Jack

Wendy Jack is a professional clairvoyant and psychic medium who works internationally, both independently and on behalf of over 14 different outlets including TV stations and magazines. Conducting spiritualist church services where she writes and delivers her written poems and positive addresses, public demonstrations, private readings, ghost hunts, house cleansing, mentoring in development circles, and writing meditations through training as a hypnotherapist. In fact, if it is spiritual, spooky, ghostly and goes bump in the night without a pulse, she's your girl! While delivering messages she uses her training as a counsellor and psychotherapist to help people on their life's pathway with compassion and guidance from her guides.

The Haunted Dolphin Hotel is her debut book where she shares not only her insight but also the experiences of many others that have sampled the 'old Dolly's' wears, as it is fondly known.

Being clairvoyant-clear seeing, clairaudience-clear hearing, clairsentience-clear feeling, clairalience-clear smelling, clairgustance-clear tasting, claircognizance-clear knowing, all through her life, Wendy's go to place was the local cemetery across the road from her childhood home, nothing weird about that then! It's the living you have to worry about not the dead! She is often quoted as saying.

Wendy lives with her teenage son, two rescue guinea pigs Fafa and Baba and two cats' lover boy Mr. Prince and prima donna she-devil Mylee, by the sea in the South of England.

Printed in Great Britain
by Amazon